Praise for *The Mental Game of Poker*

"The best poker book ever written and it's not even close."
— Lex Veldhuis, PokerStars Team Pro

"I've spent years building then blowing bankrolls online, it was only after I read Jared's book that I realized what a mental game fish I was, every chapter I read helped me fix a leak, since finishing it I haven't blown a bankroll since, it's increased both my bottom-line and love of the game."
— Niall Smyth, 2011 Irish Open Champion

"Jared has keen insight on the mental game of poker."
— Allen "The Chainsaw" Kessler

"Jared Tendler cares about people. That's why he is so good at helping them. And he can write! His book is a collection of treasures. No matter where you look, you will find riches."
— Tommy Angelo, author of *Elements of Poker*

"I'll give TMGP a big thumbs up. I think it's one of the few books that breaks new ground in the poker genre."
— Bill Rini, legendary poker blogger

"I taught a university course entitled 'Psychology of Poker' for several semesters without the benefit of an adequate textbook. Finally, Jared's book came along! Having used it twice so far, I can attest to the fact that it is the perfect blend of psychological theory and practical application. Students who diligently study this book and apply its teachings cannot help but to become successful at poker!"
— Tricia A. Cardner, PhD. EdD

"As soon as I read the book I decided we should make it the 1st book we stock in the store at Black Belt Poker. Copies have been flying off the virtual shelves like hot cakes ever since."
— Neil Channing

"I ordered *The Mental Game of Poker* and shipped my very next tourney! And the book hadn't even arrived yet! Thanks, Jared!"
— Chase Berger, "Micros"-stakes player

"The seminal work on tilt. This is no psychobabble, this is no man sitting on a leather couch in an ivory tower spewing transcendental waves. Tendler provides real steps and real answers for poker players involved in the day to day struggle who are too often beating themselves."

— Jesse May, The Voice of Poker

"Quite simply it is the only book you will ever need regarding the mental side of poker."

— Matthew Pitt, Betfair

"Best thing Jared's book did for me is show how my learning process works. After that, I got back in the right mindset and started working my ass off, with great results!"

— Steven Van Zadelhoff, Everest Poker Pro

"I'm a tilt monkey and finished the book with the confidence knowing I can diminish tilting at the tables."

— Paul "Tao Pauly" McGuire, author of Lost Vegas

"This book is the first of its kind and should be considered mandatory reading for any poker player."

— Hunter Bick, DragTheBar CEO & poker professional

"TMGOP is one of the most important and applicable poker books written in the last ten years. It should be a staple of any serious poker player's library."

— Pawel "Verneer" Nazarewicz, author of Building a Bankroll

"The book is full of so many ways to help you improve your emotional control that they are literally spilling out from the pages."

— Lee Davy, poker journalist and poker player

"Raises the bar so high for poker mindset books, other thinkers may not be able to clear it."

— Jack Welch, poker author, editor, and player

"This book made me realize the biggest problem in my game was me. Impatience, frustration, anger, and a long downswing were a vicious cycle that needed to be broken. This book is the reason that cycle has been cracked."

— Ralph Maxwell, entertainer and poker player

THE
MENTAL GAME
OF POKER

The Mental Game of Poker: Proven Strategies for Improving Tilt Control,
Confidence, Motivation, Coping with Variance, and More

Published by Jared Tendler, LLC

Printed in the United States of America

ISBN-13: 978-0-615-43613-5
ISBN-10:   0-615-43613-7

Cover and book design by theBookDesigners, www.bookdesigners.com
Jared's headshot courtesy of Naheed Choudhry

www.jaredtendlerpoker.com

THE
MENTAL GAME
OF POKER

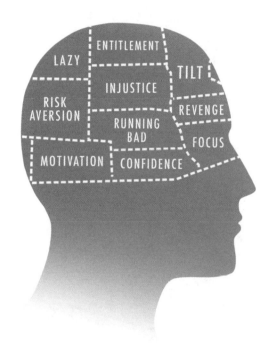

PROVEN STRATEGIES FOR IMPROVING
TILT CONTROL, CONFIDENCE, MOTIVATION,
COPING WITH VARIANCE, AND MORE

JARED TENDLER, M.S.
WITH BARRY CARTER

ACKNOWLEDGEMENTS

I've been fiercely independent throughout my life, so when I first set out to write this book, I thought I could do it on my own. I was overconfident (chapter 8). If not for the following people, this book would not have become a reality.

I'd like to thank Barry Carter, co-author, for helping turn my ideas and experience into something that would make sense to poker players. As a poker journalist, poker player, and one of the best people I know, Barry forced me to be clearer and more detailed when making a point. His enthusiasm and patience pushed me to write a better book, one that I am proud to include both of our names on. Although the original material for this book was not Barry's, his contribution was invaluable, and he made it his own. He was the perfect person to help me write the book I envisioned.

I'd like to thank my clients for sharing their stories for this book: Dusty Schmidt, Niman Kenkre, Liz Herrera, Matt Bolt, Jordan Morgan, Mike Song, Pascal Tremblay, and Sean Gibson. Your honesty and willingness to share your stories ultimately brought this book to life.

I'm also extremely grateful to *all* of my clients for giving me the opportunity to refine my method and techniques. In particular, Dusty Schmidt, my first poker client, who helped me understand the nuances of high-level poker, introduced me to the poker community, and translated my work from golf to poker.

There are a number of pioneers, such as Dr. Alan Schoonmaker, Tommy Angelo, and Matthew Hilger, who solidified the place of psychology in poker. They advanced the field and made it far easier for poker players to accept the importance of the mental game.

Without the love and ongoing support of my parents, sister, and brother-in-law, this book may never have been written. Thank you for always encouraging me to pursue my dreams, helping me persevere when it was tough, laughing at me for taking so long, and still thinking I could do it.

Thank you Corey Karsch for believing in me, lending your expert writing skills, and making the greatest accomplishment of my life more fun.

Thank you Alexis Nahoum for generously giving of your time – no questions asked. You went above and beyond, and really stepped up when I needed you. You truly helped to lighten the load, and your support and expertise were invaluable. I will be forever grateful.

A number of friends and family members also spent hours reviewing portions of this book: Jay Kotlen, Sue Kotlen, Ronit Glantz, Melissa Nagin, Ben Nagin, Paul Bacanovic, Sharon Hirshik, Andy Hirshik, and Kyra Karsch. Thank you for giving up your days, nights, and weekends to make this book easier for others to read.

Thank you David Horne, Diana Murphy, Scott Brown, Evan Rothman, Hunter Bick, *PokerNews*, Jake Poinier, and Tyler Kirkendoll. For a variety of reasons you helped make this book happen.

1

INTRODUCTION

PLAYERS WHO ARE SUCCESSFUL in the mental game of poker use a strategy that's proven to work for them. They have a structure and methodology in how they approach the mental game, and don't need to rely on a lucky rabbit's foot or praying to the poker gods.

If there were no way to control whether you play in "the zone" or go on tilt, my work as a mental game coach would be nothing more than blowing smoke up your ass. Tilting and playing your best happen for predictable reasons and occur in predictable patterns. As a poker player, you profit from your ability to analyze the patterns and habits of your opponents. Using the tools provided in this book, you will develop the ability to study the patterns and habits in your own mental game.

The fact that so many players have benefited from working on their mental game, whether from my advice or others', is proof that success in the mental game comes down to skill, as poker does. However, many players think tilt, fear, motivation, and confidence happen for random, illogical, or irrational reasons. As a result, they say or think the following:

- "Logically, I know variance happens, so it's stupid to tilt from a bad beat."

1

- "For some reason, I decided to play like a donkey last night."
- "I'm running really bad; maybe I should take a break."
- "I always play my best game on *Full Tilt*."
- "After being up big, I somehow manage to spew off a few stacks."
- "I wish I could play as well as I did today, all the time."

If you think the mental game is random, you simply lack the skill to see how it's predictable and rational.

Skilled poker players are easily able to see how the actions of weaker opponents aren't random. They pick up on betting patterns, timing tells, physical tells, and verbal tells, which allows them to exploit the games of weaker players. Weaker players don't have the skill to see the predictability in their game. The same is true in the mental game. Right now, you probably don't have the skill to recognize the actions, thoughts, and emotions that lead you to play your best or worst. That makes you a mental game fish. Thankfully, you were able to evolve from being a poker fish—and with the right information you can do the same with your mental game.

With poker more competitive than ever, more players are turning to the mental game as a valuable way to create an edge. Creating edge is not a new idea of course; it has just become more important in poker over the past several years, as the number of quality poker players has risen dramatically. Thanks to websites such as 2+2, *Cardrunners*, and others, the way the game is played has changed forever. Now, with the player pool so deep, parts of the game that weren't taken so seriously even just a few years ago, such as the mental game, are now a necessity.

Golf Sets the Stage

Athletes in all the major sports face the same challenge to stay ahead of their competition. While it's rare that a sport evolves as quickly as poker has, professional golfers recently went through something similar when Tiger Woods took the golf world by storm in the late 1990s. As he swept through the professional ranks, he brought a new set of rules that forced other professional golfers to take fitness and the mental game more seriously.

Prior to Tiger's emergence in golf, only a few of his peers looked at fitness as essential to their game. Many players were out of shape, and so golf wasn't always looked at as a *real* sport. Tiger also had a level of focus, determination, and confidence that further separated him from his competition. The combination of his physical and mental prowess forced other players on tour to follow his lead in order to remain competitive. Tiger forever changed the way professionals approached the game. Now, nearly every golfer on the PGA Tour (and other major professional tours) has a physical trainer and a sport psychologist or mental game coach. It's become the new standard.

As a successful amateur golfer in the late 1990s, I had aspirations to become a professional. There was only one big problem; I kept choking under pressure in national tournaments. One month after Tiger won his first major title, I choked trying to qualify for my first major. Shortly after completing my freshman year at Skidmore College, where I won two tournaments, I played in the first stage of qualifying for the US Open in 1997. Over the 18-hole qualifier, I played some of the best golf of my life—except on the greens. My putting was horrendous. I three-putted four times and missed several putts from short range. I shot an even par 71, and missed getting into a playoff by one shot.

It was tough coming so close, only to have my nerves get the better of me; but I wasn't going to let it stop me. I kept practicing hard, and then one day later that summer, I was describing my struggles to a friend when his eyes lit up. He knew immediately that I needed to read a book that he had just finished. He ran to the locker room and returned a few minutes later with his copy of *Golf Is Not a Game of Perfect*, by Dr. Bob Rotella. Since I knew the problem was in my head, not my swing, the book instantly resonated with me and I immediately put it into action, along with other advice I found on sport psychology. It helped, and my game continued to improve steadily over the next three years—except in big tournaments. Even though I earned All-American honors three times and won nine tournaments in college, what I learned from sport psychology didn't prevent me from choking under intense pressure.

My dreams of professional golf weren't entirely destroyed; I just had to figure out a solution to this problem. Since what was available in sport psychology at the time didn't work for me, I decided to go find my own answers. I knew I wasn't ready to play professional golf; but if I could figure out a solution, then I could play professionally and have another career option.

I suspected that conventional sport psychology was lacking an understanding of the cause of mental game problems. The traditional wisdom in golf was much as it is now in poker. I was given techniques to increase focus, increase confidence, and reduce anxiety, but I didn't learn why I choked in the first place. At the time, I believed the reason was because of personal issues that I or other golfers faced, so I enrolled in Northeastern University for a master's degree in counseling to gain that skill. Yet, what I discovered over the next 10 years is this: While personal issues certainly affect performance, mental game problems can happen for far more simple reasons; for example, hating to make mistakes, having high expectations, and having a poor work ethic.

Following my degree and 3,200 hours of supervised practice to become licensed in traditional therapy, I took what I learned and started working with golfers as a mental game coach. Over the next two and a half years, I coached more than 300, including top-ranked juniors, casual players, and professionals on the PGA Tour, Nationwide Tour, and LPGA Tour. (One player won her first tour title shortly after I started coaching her.)

Enter Poker

A stroke of good variance had me playing a round of golf at Bandon Dunes Golf Resort with Dusty "Leatherass" Schmidt in the summer of 2007. Serendipitously, I met this professional-golfer-turned-poker-pro soon after starting to play professional golf myself. From his years in golf, Dusty already knew the importance of the mental game; so when he was on the verge of his first losing month as a pro, and his pursuit of SuperNova Elite being derailed by problems with tilt, he called me for help.

Dusty was the perfect first poker client because of his background in golf. He knew my knowledge of poker was limited to home games and a few trips to Foxwoods Casino. To help me better understand poker, he often used golf terms to describe poker issues. The more we worked together, the more obvious the parallels between golf and poker became to me. The major differences are obviously the details of the game and the amount of variance. Golf has a lot of randomness—"rub of the green," as it's called—but it pales in comparison to the variance in poker. Having to sustain long stretches where skill does not equal results makes the mental game even more important in poker than in golf. It takes a strong mind to hold up during sustained bad runs, and back then, Dusty was really struggling with it.

He was a good teacher and student. Applying his well-known work ethic to his mental game, Dusty made rapid improvement in preventing tilt and quickly paid for our sessions with the savings from computer equipment (mice, keyboards, and monitors) that went unbroken. His wife even thanked me the first time we met. She could no longer tell when he won or lost.

CLIENT'S STORY

Dusty "Leatherass" Schmidt
$3/$6 to $25/$50 NLHE

POKERSTARS TEAM ONLINE PRO
Author of *Don't Listen to Phil Hellmuth*[1]
and *Treat Your Poker Like a Business*[2]

"Before I became a professional poker player, I played professional golf. As a golfer, I couldn't afford a sports psychologist, but I knew how powerful their impact was; everyone on the PGA Tour had one. I always thought there was a big correlation between poker and golf, and I figured a sports psychologist could really help my poker game, so back in 2007 I contacted Jared Tendler to help with some tilt problems.

It took a few sessions before Jared got his head around poker, but I got some real instant benefits just from talking things out, and even more once he started to understand the game. As a poker player, I'm trained to get inside the heads of others, and Jared's role was very much the same thing. The biggest impact for me was not what he said, but how he understood my thought processes. I started to realize Jared was more or less the ultimate bullshit detector, and he wasn't afraid to call me out on everything . . . I mean he literally wouldn't let me get away with anything.

Ultimately, this forced me to operate in a much more logical way. So much of what we poker players deal with is illogical, and my struggles with variance were a big example of it. Jared once asked me, 'When you look at a weather forecast and it says it's going to rain, do you get mad when you go out and it's raining? So why do you continually get angry when you know variance is going to happen?' I absolutely hate when I'm being illogical, and as soon as he reminded me that I was, I could instantly tell I was going to handle variance better.

Rather than singing some mantra, doing breathing exercises, or trying to hypnotize me not to tilt, more than anything Jared helped me just be more logical in how I approached the game. As Jared's first poker client, I am now more in the maintenance phase. When we chat, he often finds some small leaks in my mental game. I don't think anybody owns anything forever. People's mindsets change, emotions change, so working with Jared keeps me on top of my game."

1 (Imagine Media, 2011)
2 (Imagine Media, 2010)

The dramatic improvements in Dusty's mental game prompted him to try to bring me on as a featured coach on *Stoxpoker*. Since no other training website had a mental game or mindset coach at the time, it was a great opportunity to expand my practice to poker. However, I was preparing for my first full year of professional golf. I had a choice to make: pursue my dream or pursue a career? Even though I was no longer choking and was playing the best golf of my life, becoming a successful pro golfer was a huge gamble that would take years to pay off. Even though my exposure to high-level poker was limited, poker seemed like the safer bet.

I'm Not a Poker Player

"Jared Tendler invented the field as far as I'm concerned."
—Jesse May, The Voice of Poker

While I grew up playing all types of card games, including poker, high-level poker and the details of online poker were a whole new world to me. I had a lot of learning to do and I was doing it on the job. I began feverishly studying the game to better understand what poker players needed from me. Now, more than three years later, I've coached more than 170 poker players from 25 countries, and have helped thousands more by providing advice in training videos, on poker forums, and in magazine articles I've written. No one with my level of education and training has more experience working with poker players on the mental game than I do.

I'm often asked how I can help poker players when I'm a fish in most games. The best way I can explain it is with an analogy. A mechanic working on a race car doesn't need to be a world-class driver to understand how to prepare a car to win. He needs to have a deep understanding of what the driver needs, the conditions the car will race in, and how the car works, and he must be able to diagnose and fix problems quickly. Now that I understand high-level poker, I know what poker players go through, what they need to consistently perform at their best, and how to help them become mentally stronger. I'm not a poker player, but when poker players run into trouble, I'm their mechanic.

The Problem with Conventional Poker Psychology

My experience with sport psychology in the late 1990s is reflected in the comments I get now from clients about conventional poker psychology: "It helps to a point, but just doesn't stick—especially when it matters most." Most of the poker psychology I've been exposed to suggests combating bad variance and other mental game issues with general advice, deep breathing, taking breaks, visualization, meditation, Neuro-Linguistic Programming, and even hypnosis. Each of these strategies can be a great short-term option, but without resolving the underlying cause(s) of your mental game problems, they pop back up just as weeds grow back if you don't pull them out by their roots.

My experience in poker has confirmed what I found with golfers: By adopting a deeper strategy for the mental game, permanent—not just temporary—solutions can be found. What's been missing from conventional poker psychology is depth in the theory and understanding of how to develop mental game skill in a real way. Conventional wisdom knows the end game, so players are told to be fearless, to be confident, and to not let variance piss them off; but for many players that isn't enough. It's one thing to know the end game, and quite another to actually fix the problems preventing you from getting there.

Mental Game Fish

Fish are fish in part because they believe things that aren't true. They play in games where they are major underdogs without realizing it. They suck-out and believe they played great. They get schooled by another player and claim they were unlucky. They think their game doesn't need work, and even if they did, would have no idea where to start. They have no understanding of what they can and can't control at the table, and often think, "I knew the king was coming" or "I always win with ace-queen."

You may be a solid winning poker player who recognizes the shortcomings of a bad player, but as far as the mental game is concerned, you are likely no different. A solid player is a mental game fish if they:

1. Change a proven winning strategy because they are running bad/hot.
2. Never recognize when someone has played well against them and/or believe everyone they play against is bad and just gets lucky.
3. Try to win every hand.
4. Think the outcome of a hand can be changed by shouting, praying, or playing a favorite hand.
5. Get frustrated when a bad player plays badly and they even educate them as to why they are bad.
6. Feel like a failure when they lose a hand that was played profitably.
7. Think the solution to running bad is to stop playing or change stakes.
8. Read a poker book cover to cover and think they know everything in it.
9. Watch some of Phil Galfond's training videos and think they should now be able to crush the game like him.
10. Believe that they are cursed or that other people are luckier than they are.
11. Believe it's possible to own another player's soul.
12. Play more hands when they are winning/losing.
13. Play fewer hands when they are winning/losing.

14. Play badly when the stakes are too small for them to care.

15. Allow things to get personal with another regular.

16. Tell bad beat stories to anyone that will listen, while doing nothing to improve how they react to bad beats.

17. Say "one time."

Mental Game Strategy

Think of the mental game as an actual game. As with any other game, winning requires skill and a good strategy. While having a strategy is not a new idea, having a strategy for the mental game may be.

Winning in the mental game, so to speak, is fundamentally no different than learning to play winning poker: You need talent, hard work, and the right information. The only one of those you don't control is talent. Some players are just naturally more talented than you in the mental game. For example, things that piss you off barely even raise their heartbeat or they have no trouble playing poker all day, while you struggle to grind longer than an hour. Seeing the natural mental game talents of others can make it seem as if it should be easy for you too. Wrong. It's easy for them because they have more talent. Fortunately, if you are lacking talent in the mental game, hard work and the right information can eventually make it easy for you too.

Many players also believe that solutions to mental game problems are easy, because common poker wisdom makes it sound that way. So you'll hear, "Just stay calm; don't let it tilt you," "Don't focus on the money; make the right decision," or "Take a deep breath; be fearless." These all sound nice, but are the poker equivalent of saying "Just win the hand." That, of course, is the whole challenge of the game—to develop a strategy to win the hand. In the mental game, the challenge is to develop a strategy so you can remain calm, focus on the decision and not the money, and not let fear affect your decision. It's not as easy as common wisdom makes it sound.

Mental Game Myths

There are many myths about the mental game. If you're going to have real success in the mental game, you need a strategy based on sound logic and the most up-to-date research. Otherwise, you'll actually create more emotional problems and end up wasting a lot of time and effort. Your strategy is flawed if you're incorporating these common myths into your mental game:

- Emotions are a problem and need to be blocked out at all times.
- You either have mental game talent or you don't.
- Changing a habit is as simple as saying "don't do it."
- You should always quit if you think you are about to tilt.
- You can win by visualizing yourself winning.
- The key to surviving downswings is to take breaks or to drop down in stakes.
- Playing your A-game is random.
- The mental game is deep, complicated, and mysterious.

How to Use This Book

Here are some suggestions and notes about the book so you can get the most out of it.

1. **This book covers the four central areas of every poker player's mental game: Tilt, Fear, Motivation, and Confidence.** There are other areas that are important, such as focus, discipline, decision making, and playing in the zone. However, by first working on tilt, fear, motivation, and confidence, you automatically improve the other areas. The reverse is not true, which is why we start here.

2. **There is an interrelationship among issues that can be important to look at closely.** For example, motivation issues

can be caused by tilt; confidence issues can be caused by fear; tilt can be caused by confidence problems; and so on. Remember, you're a mental game fish, so don't assume you know the cause of your problem. Start with what you know and then use this book to help figure out the real problem.

3. **You may find there's a lot to work on in your mental game.** Since you can't work on everything all at once, it's important to prioritize. There are many ways to prioritize what to work on first. Here are a few:

   • Address smaller problems first because they're often the easiest to fix.

   • Fix problems that are the most costly.

   • Fix problems that happen most often.

   • Fix problems that cause the most emotional turmoil.

4. **It's like a "choose your own adventure" book.** You can skip around to chapters or sections of this book that are most relevant to you *after* you have read chapters 2, 3, and 4. Also, keep in mind that sections may not appear relevant when they actually are. Avoid discounting them too quickly.

5. **Do not read this book cover to cover and expect to know it all.** The process of improvement is more like chopping down a tree with an ax rather than cutting it down with a huge chainsaw; it happens steadily over time. Keep this book close by as you gradually and systematically work on different parts of your mental game. Mastery in any game is a moving target, so there's always something to work on in your mental game.

6. **Questions are posed to you throughout the book.** Take some time to reflect and answer these questions as if you're being asked them directly. It makes the material in the book more relevant to you, and prevents you from being tricked into thinking you

have every problem you read about. Ideally, you'll also write the answers down.

7. **When rushing to understand your mental game, it can be easy to get overloaded with information.** As it does in poker, having too much information can make you confused. Going slowly through the book, or specific sections, may make it seem like it takes longer to fix your problems, when in the long run it's often faster.

8. **Do what works.** People are diverse, so it's hard to know what's going to work best for you. Start by following the strategies provided in each chapter to gain experience. Then use your judgment to adjust your strategy to what makes sense for you. It's no different than taking a new poker concept and molding it to fit your game.

9. **Don't literally follow every word of what is written in the book.** Even if it fits you perfectly, still take a step back to think about how each point applies specifically to you. Doing so helps you learn the material and personalize the strategies.

10. **After working on your mental game in poker, you can start applying the techniques in this book to things outside of poker, such as sports, business, investing, exercise, dating, and relationships.** By also using them outside of poker, you're in effect cross-training, which helps you to learn and improve your poker mental game. That's especially true when the same problem happens in poker and outside of it.

2

FOUNDATION

ERRORS IN THE WAY players view learning and performance can cause mental game problems. When players know what to expect, they aren't fighting against what they think is true, and instead can work within the reality of what is true. Problems with tilt, fear, motivation, and confidence can be eliminated simply by better understanding how to learn and perform.

This chapter details the three theories that form the foundation of an organized and logical structure to improve your mental game. Later in the chapter, two clients describe how they used these theories to solve their tilt problem.

The three foundational theories are:

- **The Adult Learning Model:** Describes the four distinct levels of the learning process.
- **Inchworm:** Shows how improvement happens over time.
- **The Process Model:** Makes it easier to consistently play your best and improve over time.

In the short term, understanding how to better learn and perform might make things seem more complex, but in the long run you'll have the information necessary to make solving your mental game problems simpler. In addition, these three theories can be used to improve your actual poker skill.

THE ADULT LEARNING MODEL

When learning a particular skill, the process is predictable and has a distinct start and finish. While players differ in the unique aspects of learning, such as how quickly they learn, what comes easily to them, and where they get stuck, the overall process is exactly the same.

The "Adult Learning Model[1]" (ALM) is a straightforward theory that defines the four distinct levels of the learning process. The four levels are:

> **Level 1 — Unconscious Incompetence.** You don't even know what you don't know. In other words, you're blind to the ways that you lack skill, which isn't necessarily good or bad. For some players ignorance is bliss.
>
> **Level 2 — Conscious Incompetence.** Now you've become conscious of what you don't know. But that doesn't make you skilled, it just means you know what skills you need to improve. Becoming conscious happens from either your own insight or insight that is shared with you by someone else.
>
> **Level 3 — Conscious Competence.** If you've reached this level, it means you've done some work

---

1   The origin is uncertain. Attribution is often given to Abraham Maslow, as well as Dr. Thomas Gordon. It's also known as the Four Stages of Learning or the Conscious Competency Model. Cited in: McHugh, Donald E. 2004. Golf and the game of leadership: an 18-hole guide for success in business and life. New York, NY: AMACOM.

and/or have had enough repetition to gain some skill. The only catch is that in order to be skilled, you need to think about what you've learned . . . otherwise, you return to being incompetent.

Level 4 — Unconscious Competence. At this level, you've learned something so well that it is now totally automatic and requires no thinking. Unconscious Competence is the Holy Grail of learning, and by far the most important concept in this book.

These levels make sense when you begin to think about your own experiences in learning poker or just about anything else. A familiar example that shows the ALM in action is learning to drive a car.

Remember when you were a small child thinking about driving a car. You barely knew what a car was, let alone how to drive one. This is Unconscious Incompetence. Then as a teenager, you became much more aware of driving and perhaps were frustrated by the fact that you couldn't drive. You became conscious of your incompetence.

Now think back to when you got behind the wheel for the first time. In order to drive a car, you first needed to learn how to: steer, step on the gas, watch the road, and change the radio station all at the same time; parallel park; adjust to the speed of highway traffic; and deal with thousands of unique situations. Then, you needed to concentrate and think about all of these things so you didn't kill yourself or others. This is Conscious Competence.

After driving for years, you no longer think about every single action needed to drive a car; your skill comes naturally and with little effort. You can handle driving, listening to music, talking to passengers, and extreme situations that arise, such as adverse weather, all without much thought. Driving is a skill now trained to the level of Unconscious Competence.

To begin looking at how the ALM applies to poker, take a minute to think about:

1. How much you knew the first time you played poker.

2. The complexity of your thought process when making poker decisions now compared to when you first started really trying to improve.

3. A mistake you recently discovered.

4. Decisions at the table that are made automatically.

5. Mistakes that don't happen anymore.

FLAWS ARE SKILLS

Within your Unconscious Competence are also flaws or old habits in your technical poker game as well as your mental game. Basically, you're really good at these bad habits, but you no longer want to be.

A good example from poker that demonstrates the levels of the ALM is starting hand selection. When playing for the first time, you may not even have been aware of the concept and played too many hands. Even with some knowledge of starting hands, the first time you played it's unlikely you had any clue of why calling a 3-bet out of position with QJo is a mistake. So, whether you were unconsciously incompetent about the concept as a whole, or just the finer details, in some way this was a weakness and you didn't know it.

Fast forward to a few weeks or months after you started learning more about how to play poker, and specifically hand selection. You may have picked up information about it from a friend or book that advocates the value of certain hands from certain positions, from an opponent who berated you for playing QJo, or from playing more you started to realize you were second best far too often. You weren't sure what hands you should be playing yet, but you did realize something was off. Simply realizing that you were making mistakes in hand selection didn't mean you were good at it, just that you needed to work on it. An easy way to know that you're at the level of Conscious Incompetence is that you've recognized a mistake for the first time.

After playing and studying more, you know the pluses and minuses of all the possible starting hands. It feels as if you're improving; you're in control of the hands you're playing and things are good . . . until you lose focus at the end of a long session or you're frustrated having lost a few big pots . . . now suddenly you fall back into old habits and start playing hands you know you shouldn't. The mistakes are obvious afterward, but that only reinforces the reality that you actually don't know the correct hands to play as well as you thought. At this point in the learning process, you still need to think about which hands to play, otherwise you make mistakes.

After more experience, more work, and more learning, your job is finally complete. Now, when you're dealt marginal hands, even on tilt, you muck them without a thought, an insta-fold. It's a new habit or decision made automatically. A lot of work is needed to get here, and the benefit is well worth it. Now you no longer need to think about starting hands to be good at it, and because of that, your mind is free to learn something new.

Whether it's starting hands or tilt control, there is a limit to how much your mind can think about in a given moment. You can only work on parts of your game at one time. As a result, it's critical to know the level of the ALM your skills are in, so you know what to focus on improving. If you no longer need to think to be good, you have more mental space to work on another weakness in your game, and move it eventually from Conscious Incompetence to the level of Unconscious Competence. However, if you fall back into old habits, you clearly need more work no matter what you thought.

In reality, the learning process has many more small steps than the ALM specifies—but as an overall theory, it's brilliantly simple and incredibly important to your game.

INCHWORM

"Inchworm" is a concept with a strange name that helps make the process of improving over time easier to understand. Inchworm isn't a revolutionary new idea; it's just an observation of how you improve over time and something you likely never thought about previously. Understanding this concept more clearly will help you to:

- Become more efficient in your approach to improving.
- Make consistent improvement while avoiding common pitfalls.
- Avoid fighting a reality you can't change.
- Know where a skill is in the learning process.
- Handle the natural ups and downs of learning better.

There will be times when it feels like you have taken a huge step backward, not progressed at all, or fallen back into old habits. The next time this happens, come back to this section.

Understanding the concept of inchworm starts by looking more closely at the natural range that exists in the quality of your poker or mental game. Think for a moment about the quality of your poker decisions when playing your absolute best and when playing at your worst. In other words, how good does it get when you're playing great, and how bad does it get when you're playing poorly?

To illustrate a point, let's say you rated the quality of every decision you made at the poker table (your best, worst, and everything in between) over the last 6 to 12 months on a scale of 1 (worst) to 100 (best) and plotted them on a graph. What you'd see on that graph is a bell curve.

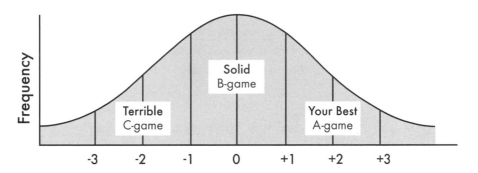

The right or positive side represents your best decisions.
The left or negative side represents your worst decisions.

This bell curve shows the natural range that exists in your game and the game of every poker player on the planet—even shortstackers (although theirs is the narrowest). As long as you're playing poker, you'll always have aspects of your game that represent the peak of your ability, and the flip side, your worst. Always. Perfect poker isn't possible over a large number of hands. There are times you play perfectly and other times that you don't. Poker is a dynamic game that's becoming more competitive. This means that the definition of perfection, even just solid play, is a moving target. As long as your game evolves, that means you're learning. If you're learning, that means there's range in the quality of your decision making.

Poker isn't the only instance where range exists. It's everywhere you look, especially in professional sports. Take any player in a major professional sport and evaluate the quality of their skill set over a large enough sample and you'll see a bell curve. Baseball players hit home runs and make diving catches, as well as strike out and make errors. Quarterbacks throw perfect forty-yard passes into tight coverage and then throw terrible interceptions. Soccer players make sharp passes to set up an incredible goal and also whiff or shank the ball.

When looking more closely at your game, for better or worse, it's important to be honest about the reality of the range that exists. Not what you wish the reality to be, but what it actually is. Take a look at the strengths in your decision making, represented by the right side of your bell curve. These are decisions that happen when your thinking is perfect, so they come easily because you have a solid understanding of your opponents and you're in the flow of the game. Generally, you have a great mindset and are in the zone.

The right side also includes new information gained from your own insights, training videos, talking with other players, etc., which allows you to make even better decisions than usual. Remember, these are skills at the level of Conscious Competence and cannot yet be counted as a solid part of your game.

On the other side of the bell curve are all of the terrible decisions you make. These are all the mistakes you know you shouldn't be making, but still do. Often these are directly connected to mental game problems, such as your mind going blank in a huge pot and folding the obvious best hand; misreading an opponent because you're bored and your terrible bluff gets called; or tilting and play too many hands way too aggressively. Clearly, these are all the things you want out of your game because they not only cost a lot of money, but they create more frustration, confusion, and confidence problems. This book is designed to help you improve the back end of your mental game range, which means that not only will these obvious poker mistakes go away, you'll also play closer to your mental peak more frequently.

The concept of inchworm comes in when you look at how the range in your poker game or mental game improves over time. A bell curve is a snapshot of a given sample, while improvement is the movement of a bell curve over time; something an actual inchworm illustrates perfectly in the way it moves.

An inchworm looks like a bell curve.

If you've never seen the way an inchworm moves, it starts by stretching its body straight, anchors the front "foot," then lifts up from the back end, bends at the middle to bring the two ends closer together, anchors the back foot, then stretches its body straight again, and takes another step forward.

When you reach a new peak in your ability, the front end of your range takes a step forward. Your best just became better, which also means that your range has widened because the worst part of your game hasn't moved yet. The most efficient way to move forward again is to turn your focus to the back end of your range and make improvements to your greatest weaknesses. By eliminating what is currently the worst part of your game, your bell curve takes a step forward from the back end, and now it's easier to take another step forward from the front.

The inchworm concept illustrates how consistent improvement happens by taking one step forward from the front of your bell curve followed by another step forward from the back. The implications of this concept are that:

1. Improvement happens from two sides: improving weakness and improving your best.

2. Playing your best is a moving target, because it's always relative to the current range in your game.

3. You create the potential for an even greater A-game when you eliminate your mental and poker C-games because mental space is freed up to learn new things. (Yes, the quality of your mental peak or zone can actually improve as well.)

CLIENT'S STORY

Niman "Samoleus" Kenkre
5/10 to 25/50 NLHE

BLUEFIRE POKER COACH

"It's kind of unusual; I actually started talking with Jared when I was on a real tear, and at the top of my game. I'd been a successful pro for more than five years, but had a really rough patch at the end of 2009. I was playing really poorly and was screwed up a bit mentally. I sorted my game out on my own and went to Jared when I was playing well, because I thought in a better state of mind I would get more out of it. Plus, I figured working with him might prevent my game from slipping again.

I was really skeptical working with a mental game coach; what was he going to tell me that I hadn't heard before? I expected goofy stuff like 'stay calm,' 'don't worry about results,' 'visualize yourself winning,' blah, blah, blah—stuff you read in forums. I was really surprised; Jared has a fantastic system of learning and it had a really immediate and emphatic effect on me.

He talked about concepts, such as inchworm, in a context that I never thought about. Realizing how the front end fits with my back end was eye-opening. I always thought of my A-game and my F-game as two separate things. Jared helped me understand how they worked together, which made it very systematic and clear how to improve myself overall as a player. I now understand that when I am playing my worst game, I have to work hard to make it a little better, so it won't be as bad tomorrow.

I also didn't understand how emotions were part of the learning model. Surprisingly, just knowing more about that completely removed the effect negative emotions had on my play. Previously, I would take bad beats and have bad players get rewarded, and I'd react like a caveman – 'that guy was stealing my money!!!' I didn't have a framework to understand those emotions, and then everything would go haywire. The whole concept of Unconscious Competence helped to totally change all that, as well as how I went about working on my game.

Unconscious Competence may be the single most important thing Jared taught me. When I was on tilt, one of my leaks would be that I would get frustrated when players 3-bet me in position with hands they *should not* be playing. I would overplay my hands, and get really tilted at how they were playing. It was my weakest area, and I knew I wasn't playing well, but couldn't wrap my head around it. Jared laughed and asked, 'So your opponents are not allowed to play in a way that puts you at your weakest?' Seeing it in that context made me realize instantly that my emotional reaction was trying to protect my greatest weakness. I fixed the leak, and now when I encounter those situations my head is much better. It's still frustrating, but my play doesn't go haywire, because playing well in that situation is now learned to the level of Unconscious Competence.

Now, every day that I play, I think of my play in the context of the learning model. My tilt-induced emotions come up far less frequently, and when they do come up, they don't affect my play as much as they used to. That's another important thing I took away from Jared. After a couple sessions, I assumed I was supposed to have this Zen-like state of mind and shouldn't get tilted by bad beats because I now 'understood.'

Emotions are going to be there and just knowing that makes them easier to handle. I've been a pro poker player now for five years, and there has been no greater positive influence on my game than my lessons with Jared, and nothing else even comes close."

Two Common Learning Mistakes

To further understand how inchworm applies specifically to poker, here are two common mistakes players often make, along with a solution for each:

Ignoring weaknesses. When players constantly learn new things while avoiding, ignoring, blocking out, or protecting weaknesses, their bell curve gets flatter and flatter. Weaknesses haven't improved, so the back end doesn't move. They also have a bunch of new skills to use, so when they're at their best, they're better than ever. The problem is that by exclusively learning new things, they create a wide range in their game, which means that it takes a lot of mental effort to think through all these new concepts.

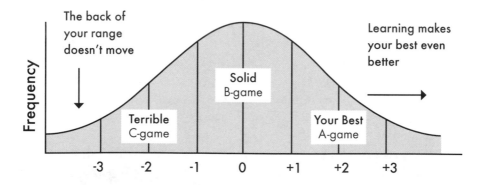

If you aren't mentally sharp, there's a dramatic drop-off in your play. So when you're at your best, you're better than ever; but when your play goes bad, it gets really bad.

Here are a few other consequences for this approach to learning:

- Playing your best takes a lot of energy so it doesn't happen that often.

- Mistakes, many of them basic, show up completely out of nowhere.

- It feels as if you've stopped improving and your game has plateaued.

- You have a lot to think about and often get confused or miss important details of a hand.

To make matters worse, all the new information you've acquired is in the process of being learned, so it won't show up when you go on tilt, lose focus, get tired, or are nervous in a huge pot. When any of those mental game problems happen, it feels as if you've just had the carpet yanked out from under you—and now you're lying on the floor (the back side of your bell curve) with your confidence shattered, wondering what the hell happened. For some players, this leads them to question everything in their game, which accelerates the free-fall like an airplane in a death spiral.

The consequence of not working on your weaknesses and exclusively learning new things could be the difference between being a slight loser and a solid winner. Preventing this from happening is actually quite simple: You must stay focused on learning the correction to your weaknesses until it is trained to the level of Unconscious Competence—especially after your A-game improves. Doing so keeps you humble, reminds you of your weaknesses, and is the most efficient way for your best to improve.

Comparing your worst to your best. Inchworm also has another important lesson that comes in handy when your game is under pressure from being on a bad run, on tilt, or having poor motivation and focus. During these times, it's especially hard to maintain proper perspective, especially for improvement in your poker and mental games. While actually recognizing improvement may not seem like much, it can be critical to helping turn things around.

The only way that you can prove the back end of your game has taken a step forward is by analyzing your game at its worst, and comparing it with your worst during a previous tough stretch. So, rather than comparing your game at its worst to your recent peak, which can seem miles away and makes you feel worse, instead compare apples to apples, or your worst to your previous worst. Remember, it's under intense pressure that you rely heavily on skills at the level of Unconscious Competence; so for better or worse, what shows up at that point gives you a perfect view of the greatest weaknesses in your game.

Comparing your worst to your previous worst allows you to prove that the back end of your range has improved. For example, you might not be completely tilt-free, but compared to before you are more aware of your tilt pattern, manage your tilt better so you play better longer, and quit sooner when it's no longer possible to recover a solid thought process. Basically, you're looking to see your worst improve; and seeing that you have improved in the midst of a tough stretch can give you a much-needed confidence boost.

THE PROCESS MODEL

"The process model" organizes the naturally recurring parts of your entire poker game so you can put the principles of the ALM and inchworm into action day after day. The net result is consistently playing at a high level, while also making steady improvement in your poker and mental games. The process model also applies to a single hand, a single session or tournament, a month of playing, a year, or a career.

The process model doesn't invent anything new, but it provides some order to things you already do, creates a foundation to achieve mastery, improves results-oriented thinking, and ultimately leads to more consistent play.

The process model has five parts that all work together:

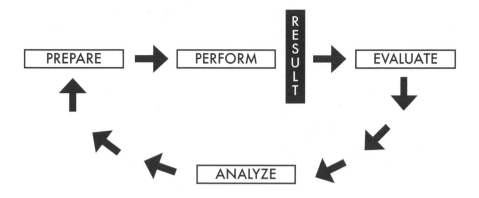

1. **Preparation/Warm-up:** What you do before you play. Whether it's planned, random, or nothing at all, it's how you prepare.

2. **Performance:** Playing poker.

3. **Results:** The outcome of your play.

4. **Evaluation:** A review of your results right after playing.

5. **Analysis:** Actively working to improve your game away from the table.

The process model is something that applies to anything in life involving performance. You've already used it in countless areas of your life, such as sports, dating, music, art, writing, business, and of course, poker. Even if you weren't aware at the time that you were using the process model, in some way you were.

Here is a more detailed look at the process model when it is applied to professional (American) football and poker:

Preparation/Warm-up

In professional football, preparation starts shortly after the last game, and ends just before kickoff. Throughout the week, coaches and players review game tape, run drills, lift weights, analyze opponents, formulate a strategy, and practice that strategy—all with the intent of getting ready to play at a high level and win. The day of the game, the players and coaches follow a structured routine to warm up their bodies, focus their minds, and review their tactical strategy so they're ready to compete. They run drills, rehearse plays, listen to music, double-check equipment, and fire each other up.

While the details are very different in poker, the intent of preparation remains the same: to be ready to perform at your best and win. Part of the reason preparation is so important in poker is because of the range that exists in the quality of your game. Every time you sit down to play, you could play great, or you could play terribly. Preparation provides a way to make it more likely that you'll perform in the front end of your ability, and less likely that your worst will show up.

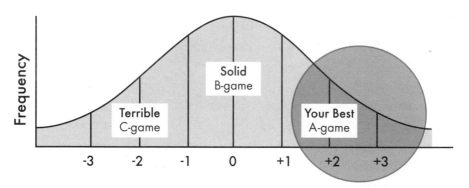

Preparation makes you more likely to perform at your best (front end of your range) and puts you in a position to play better than ever.

How you prepare is a matter of personal preference that is based on your overall goals. There are no hard-and-fast rules for what makes preparation ideal, because ultimately it's all about doing what makes the most sense for you.

Here are some general things you can do to prepare to play:

- Review your long-term goals and set goals for the session.
- Review a list with the corrections to your common poker mistakes.
- Review your strategy for improving mental game issues.
- Use deep breathing, meditation, and/or visualization to steady and focus your mind.
- Listen to a favorite song.

For more instructions on how to prepare, go to Appendix I.

CLIENT'S STORY

Dusty "Leatherass" Schmidt
$3/$6 to $25/$50 NLHE

POKERSTARS TEAM ONLINE PRO
Author of *Don't Listen to Phil Hellmuth*
and *Treat Your Poker Like a Business*

"Before I started working with Jared, I didn't warm-up before I played, which made me much more vulnerable to the effects of a downswing. I really didn't want to get upset if I had a bad run; getting upset would make me stupid, and I didn't want to be stupid. More than anything, I didn't want to get called out on my bullshit again by Jared. So we developed a pre-game routine that prepared me for a bad run.

The warm up is essential. I always knew how detrimental it would be for me not to warm-up before a golf tournament; really, I never even thought about not doing it. Now I feel the same way about poker. This was proven to me recently when I got on some waiting lists before I had warmed up properly. Seats started popping up; seats that happened

THE MENTAL GAME OF POKER

to be the Jesus seats you can't pass up, so f*&% the mental routine, I started playing.

Within the first 5 to 10 minutes, my hand on the mouse started shaking. I know from years of experience that I only tend to get nervous when I don't know what I'm doing. In golf that happens when my putting stroke gets off and I am under tournament pressure. I'm loosey-goosey when I know what I'm doing, but my hand started shaking that day at the tables because I hadn't prepared and wasn't mentally ready to deal with terrible cards. I didn't play my best and the session snowballed. No matter what, I always warm up now."

Performance

In football, playing the game is the players' and coaches' only opportunity to put their skills and hard work to the test. Their performance includes everything from the first play of the game to the last.

Performance in poker is just as obvious and doesn't need to be repeated. However, what isn't obvious are the consequences when preparation or evaluation occurs while you're playing.

Ideally, preparation has you ready to play at a high level from the start of your session. If you do nothing to prepare beforehand, the beginning of the session is your preparation. That may mean you'll play marginally for the first 10 to 15 minutes until your mind is fully into the action. Consequently, you're less focused—and you make mistakes, you fail to pick up reads on an opponent that set up future mistakes, and became susceptible to other mental game problems.

Ideally, evaluation only happens after the session when you can objectively look closely at how you played. (This is typically more relevant online than live.) However, players often review hands in the middle of a session, fixate on past hands looking for mistakes, run equity calculations, and check Hold'em Manager or PokerTracker. Basically, they are evaluating how they are playing while they are playing. In other words, they're multitasking, and they play worse for that reason alone.

Removing evaluation doesn't mean eliminating adjustments. Adjusting to your opponents is how you stay at least one step ahead of them while you're playing. Adjustments are key; evaluating while playing is excessive. If you are spending too much time reviewing previous hands, your adjustments aren't known well enough. Ideally, they should be so well known that they are made automatically and without thought (Unconscious Competence). Otherwise, you're no different from a quarterback making up a play at the line of scrimmage rather than calling an audible (a pre-determined alternate play his teammates already know well). Instead of evaluating, mark the hand or take a quick note, and refocus on the action.

RESULTS-ORIENTED THINKING

Not being results-oriented gets a lot of attention in the poker world these days. The solution most often given is to ignore, block out, or detach from your results. Players know it's a mistake to focus too much on short-term results because of variance, but stopping is easier said than done. When you only focus on wins and losses, your emotions go on a rollercoaster because they are attached to money and winning. Being focused on winning and money in the short run is not what causes problems; it's the set of results you're ignoring.

You also need to focus on qualitative results so your emotions can attach to factors that you have 100% control of in the short run. The process model provides the structure and organization to capture qualitative results since they aren't easily calculated at the end of a session or tournament. Use the model to focus more and more on the quality of your play, your mental game, and overall improvement; and steadily your emotions will reorganize around this set of results.

Results

In both football and poker, there are many ways to measure the outcome of a player's performance. Typically, poker players think of results mainly in terms of things easily quantified, such as money, wins and losses, number of hands and hours played, and win rate. However, it's also essential to account for qualitative results, such as how well you played, your level of focus, the degree of tilt control, and your improvement of weaknesses.

Evaluation

The first opportunity to gain an objective view about what happened during play is immediately after you finish playing. When you're actually playing—whether it's football or poker—you play your best by focusing intensely on the game itself and far less on how you are playing.

After football games, the media instantly rush over to speak with players and coaches to get their reactions. What they share is a quick snapshot of a few things they noticed or how they feel in the moment, but not solid details. Once back in the locker room, players talk with each other and have more time to reflect on the game. Coaches also start a formal review of player performance, going through game tape and reviewing their own decisions to get an initial impression of what needs work before the next game.

Poker players tend to overly focus on money immediately after a session because it matters most in the long run, and it's so easy to calculate. The problem is that because of variance, monetary results alone are unreliable measures in the short term of how you played. Here are a few better ways to evaluate how you played:

- Look closely at tough decisions to see how you played them.
- Estimate how much variance influenced results.
- Calculate whether you accomplished the qualitative goals you set before the session. If you fell short, why?

- Review how you did in the areas you're trying to improve (poker strategy and mental game). Did you see any progress?
- If you're going to analyze hands later, write some game flow notes or thoughts about them that you may otherwise forget.

Spending a short time to evaluate is also a great way to:

- Put poker down when you're done playing, so you can go on with your life.
- Reset your mind before the next time you play.

CLIENT'S STORY

Niman "Samoleus" Kenkre
$5/$10 to $25/$50 NLHE

BLUEFIRE POKER COACH

"I don't use a HUD, but have always kept a spreadsheet for tax purposes. In addition to putting in amount of time, stakes, and net profit for the day, I also have a column for my comments, which previously had just been things like, 'Stupid freakin' donkey sucked out on me.' After working with Jared, I now have two other columns. One is a rating where I evaluate the quality of my play, and the other is a comment about the quality of how I handled my emotions. Now I find myself striving to play and manage my emotions really well. I am less focused on my profit and more on my rating; I want to be able to put a 9 or 9.5 for my play, and that's how I now define my success. I find myself being able to do that honestly; for example, I had a losing session a couple of days ago but felt I played tremendously well. I gave myself a high rating and walked away from the day feeling very good."

Analysis

Analysis is the stage where you actively work on your game away from the action. It's the best time to go into greater detail assessing your play and your opponents' play, as well as bring in additional resources to ensure you're a stronger player.

In football, this includes a more detailed analysis of the game tape, such as scrutinizing the mistakes a quarterback made in reading the defense can be scrutinized. Perhaps an audible was mistakenly called because he saw something that didn't actually happen. While watching the game tape and reviewing his decision-making process, he can figure out what went wrong and then use the week leading up to the next game to fix it. Doing this kind of tedious work isn't necessarily the most fun part of a player's week, but it is often the most valuable.

In poker, analysis doesn't have to be done immediately after sessions; in fact, sometimes it's best to take a break before diving in. There are many ways to work on your game, such as analyzing marked hands, posting on and reading forums, watching training videos, doing equity calculations, talking with other players, and studying regulars.

After you're done analyzing, take what you've learned and adjust your preparation or warm-up to include the most up-to-date information. That way, you're even better prepared the next time you play.

Use the Process Model Every Day

Ultimately, the process model makes your approach to performance and improvement more active, organized, measurable, and efficient. When you use it over long stretches of time, you also improve your ability to learn and achieve results. Too often, players only start working hard on their game when they're running bad, playing poorly, or their win rate drops. Why wait until something negative happens? With poker more competitive, players gain an advantage by continually learning and improving. Use the process model every day you play to keep your learning curve steadily rising, so your game never plateaus.

3

EMOTION

EMOTION IS NOT THE PROBLEM. It's the key to mastering your game.

The fundamental difference between the common approaches to poker psychology and this book comes down to how emotion is viewed. When emotion is viewed as the cause of problems at the poker table, it makes perfect sense why conventional wisdom would urge you to become robotic, trick your mind, or become desensitized to emotion. In essence, traditional tactics are suggesting that anger, fear, and overconfidence are inherently bad, so you must get rid of them. Of course, your end goal is to get these negative emotions out of your game, but they are the symptom—not the true cause of why you play poorly.

Finding the cause of your emotional problems requires digging a little deeper, and when you do, the role of emotion completely changes. Emotion, once seen as the problem, now serves a valuable purpose: highlighting flaws in how you are mentally approaching the game. In essence, emotion is a messenger telling you exactly what to work on in your mental game. (If you have no idea what the messenger is saying, you try to kill it.)

Emotions that cause problems in your game are created when flaws in your approach to poker are triggered by certain events or occurrences at the table. Let's take a bad beat for example. A bad beat does not cause tilt. If it did, then every player would have the exact same reaction to one, but some players continue to play well no matter how many bad beats they take. Thus, it can't be the nature of a bad beat that causes tilt; tilt must be caused by something else. It's caused by a flaw in a player's approach to poker, such as a form of entitlement where a player believes he's too good to lose to a weaker player. When that player, with that belief, takes a bad beat from a weaker player, he predictably becomes angry. So a bad beat causes anger only when that flaw (or others like it) exists within a player's mental game.

Resolution

When you view emotion as the symptom and not the problem, an entirely new solution to mental game problems emerges: "resolution." Resolution keeps all the positive features that emotions add to your game and removes the negatives. When you resolve the underlying cause of negative emotions, such as anger and fear, they disappear. Resolution may sound like a strange idea, but it's something you've already done, and may regularly do without even realizing it.

Resolving mental game flaws is how you become mentally strong. Players often talk about this concept, but few understand how to truly build mental muscle. Instead, they believe mental strength happens simply by taking on a certain mindset. That perceived strength is temporary because you're essentially pretending that underlying flaws don't exist. So you feel confident, fearless, or tilt-free for a short time, but whatever mental strength you feel is really an illusion. The flaws are still there, hidden in the background, until they pop back up and take your mental game by surprise.

Achieving resolution means developing real mental strength. While resolution can be complex, this entire book is organized around making it as straightforward as possible. *For detailed steps to resolve your mental game problems, go to page 59.*

Malfunctioning Mind

There is one basic brain function that is not well-known by poker players, or even by the general public. Failing to understand it directly impacts your attempts to control and fix emotional problems.

First, here's a little background information to help you understand how the brain works. The brain is organized in a hierarchy. The first level is where all of the most important functions of the brain are stored, such as heart rate, breathing, balance, and sleep/wake cycles. Unconscious Competence is also there. The second level of the brain is the emotional system, and the third is the mental level containing all of the higher brain functions, such as thinking, planning, perception, awareness, organization, and emotional control. Here's the rule:

When the emotional system becomes overactive, it shuts down higher brain functions.

Translation: If your emotions are too high, you make poor poker decisions because the brain prevents you from being able to think straight. The following also happens:

- Your mind goes blank.

- You miss key pieces of the hand.

- You overweight the importance of some information, or fixate on irrelevant information.

- You know the right answer, but it's as if your head is in a fog.

- You fall back into bad habits.

Unfortunately, when emotions are overactive, the loss of higher brain functions is something that no one controls. It's a hardwired part of our brain that isn't going to change. Many of you know it as the "fight or flight response," and your mind is essentially malfunctioning as if it were a computer short-circuiting.

While you can't control the fact that the emotional system shuts down your ability to think, once you see the two implications of this rule, it's easier to gain control of your emotions and therefore improve your mental game.

First, you must start trying to control your emotions before reaching your emotional threshold (the point where emotions start to shut down higher brain functions); otherwise, you're fighting an uphill battle. Too often, mental game strategies suggest that it's easy to think when you're on tilt. It's not. Your brain shuts off your ability to think.

Second, when you combine this rule with the ALM, you get a perfect snapshot of the skills in your Unconscious Competence. When your emotions are too high and you can't think, you lose access to the skills that you are currently in the process of learning—Conscious Competence.[1] So what's left? Unconscious Competence. When you go on tilt or are nervous in a big pot, the knowledge or skill that you use to make poker decisions *only* comes from your Unconscious Competence. It's for this reason that your decisions are so poor compared to what you expect; everything that is currently being learned doesn't show up. *To better understand how this can actually benefit your game, go to pages 75 and 150.*

Two Causes of Emotion

In the introduction to this chapter, emotion is described as being caused by flaws in your Unconscious Competence triggered by such things as bad beats, mistakes, and losing. There is another place where emotion is created that is important to account for: the mind.

---

1   You don't lose all of your Conscious Competency skills because the amount of thinking lost is in direct proportion to your level of emotion. Meaning, the higher your level of emotion is past the threshold, the less you can think.

Emotion produced from two places

When you become aware of anxiety, anger, or low motivation, the mind can make that emotion multiply. So you get more anxious because you're already anxious; you tilt harder because you recognize that you're angry; your motivation decreases because you're aware of how little you already have. These extra layers increase the amount of emotion you need to deal with, and they make it harder for you to remain in control.

Accumulated Emotion
Normally, the accumulation of emotion rises and falls within a given day. After a day when you lose a bunch of money, the frustration that built up during the session starts to disappear once you're done playing, and eventually fades away entirely. For some players, all of the frustration may be gone within a few minutes, or on a really tough day it could take a few hours, along with a workout at the gym, before it's completely gone. Either way, the next time you sit down to play, it's as if the frustration never existed.

However, sometimes emotion doesn't completely disappear. So the next time you play you aren't starting from scratch; there's still some residual emotion hanging around from the last time you played. It may not seem like much, but this extra emotion (tilt, overconfidence, doubt) means that your threshold has lowered and less emotion than normal needs to accumulate before you cross it. Consequently, you tilt quicker, you protect a win faster, or your mind goes blank after playing fewer big pots.

Emotion accumulating like this over several days is what makes it difficult to play well when running bad or running good. As the run goes on, it becomes tougher and tougher for the brain to completely reset itself from the emotion created in previous sessions. It accumulates bit by bit, day by day, until tilt instantly happens from the first lost hand, or you quit instantly after winning a couple buy-ins, fearing you'll lose it back.

Emotion can also accumulate over weeks, months, and years around a particular issue. Let's take a player who believes he always runs bad, or never gets his fair share of the luck.[2] As the months and years go on, his anger gets stronger and stronger when he loses flips, or a fish sucks-out in a big pot. This "emotional baggage," as it's often called, weighs down heavily on his mind and causes him to react in a way that seems totally disproportionate to what happened. Losing a standard coin flip sends him on insane tilt because he is reacting to *all* the coin flips he's lost in the past—not just this one.

This "accumulated emotion" or emotional baggage is the toughest part of the mental game to improve. The reason is that you have to contend with the emotion created today from losing, mistakes, or running hot, *plus* you have to contend with the lingering emotion created by these issues over time. When set off, the intensity is so strong that it quickly overwhelms your mind and your ability to remain in control; so you instantly tilt, mentally freeze in a big pot, or believe you're a poker god. The *only* way you can stay in control at that time is by doing work off the table to reduce accumulated emotion.

Conceptually, the work required away from the table to resolve accumulated emotion is no different from working on a complex area of

---

2   Probably a bad example since this kind of player is so rare in poker?!

technical poker knowledge that you can't do while playing, such as complex equity or ICM calculations. *For more on resolving accumulated emotion, go to page 66.*

Spectrum of Emotion

Emotion exists along a spectrum that increases in intensity as it accumulates. Each of the four major emotions covered in this book—anger, fear, motivation, and confidence—have spectrums:

- Anger runs from minor frustration to insane monkey tilt.
- Fear runs from uncertainty to major phobia.
- Motivation runs from lazy and hopeless to highly inspired.
- Confidence runs from a total lack of confidence to being an over-confident poker god.

While this may not be earth-shattering news, emotions that exist along the same spectrum often appear to be separate and random. Instead, by organizing emotions on the appropriate spectrum, accumulation of a particular emotion becomes easier to recognize. The better you can recognize when emotion accumulates, the better you can take action to prevent it from crossing the threshold and remain in total emotional control.

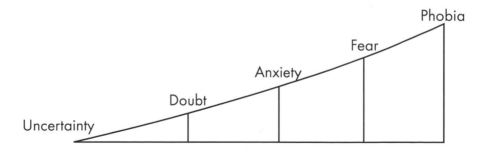

Doubt, anxiety, fear, and phobia are the accumulation of uncertainty over time.

Here's an example of how emotion builds along a spectrum: A player might have some uncertainty after a rough, losing day, unsure if he played badly or if it was just variance. Then, after a few more days of constantly running into the top end of players' ranges, he begins to doubt if he's making the right plays. He starts to hesitate, second-guess decisions, go against his gut, and make mistakes. Then, anxiety starts showing up in bigger pots because he's afraid of making a mistake. Eventually, these mistakes do happen because his mind is malfunctioning. Now, with bad play mixed into the bad run, anxiety starts to build before even sitting down to play. Simply thinking about playing is enough to spark anxiety. Over time, what started as uncertainty has turned into a strong fear of losing. So, he doesn't play as much and instead spends hours working on his game trying to figure out how to play perfectly and avoid losing.

Performance and Emotion

Emotion is essential for performance. It's only when there is too much or too little emotion that there is a problem. This is true of both positive emotions and negative emotions. Having too much confidence is a problem because it shuts down your ability to think. Being tired is a problem because you don't have enough energy to think.

Understanding the relationship between emotion and performance, as shown by the following principle, makes improving your mental game easier. Yerkes-Dodson Law[3] describes the relationship between the level of arousal (the psychological term for energy, emotion, focus, or stress) and a player's performance. This law states that your performance improves as your emotions rise . . . but only to a certain point.

---

3   Yerkes RM, Dodson JD (1908). "The relation of strength of stimulus to rapidity of habit-formation." *Journal of Comparative Neurology and Psychology* 18: 459–482.

Yerkes-Dodson Law

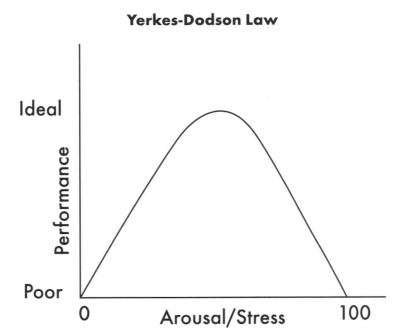

If emotion continues to rise and crosses your threshold (the top of the curve), performance starts to decline because the emotional system shuts down your ability to think. You can't perform as well because you can't think as well; and if you can't think as well, you can't access the skills you're currently learning.

On the left side of the curve, the opposite thing happens. When you don't have enough emotion to think, as occurs when you're tired or unmotivated, you need to build up enough energy to get the thinking part of your brain into gear. Otherwise, you'll play just as poorly as if you were on tilt.

The general strategy outlined in the next chapter is designed to help keep your emotional level at the top of the performance curve. This allows you to play your best poker more often, while resolving the mental game problems that create havoc in your game.

4

STRATEGY

THE FIRST THREE CHAPTERS of this book set the stage for the general strategies described in this chapter. Since the four central areas of your mental game—tilt, fear, motivation, and confidence—play by the same rules, similar strategies are used to address them. This chapter lays out a logical, organized, and strategic approach to resolving mental game problems. In the remaining chapters, you'll find additional strategies and advice specific to each issue.

The two primary strategies needed for solving mental game problems are:

1. **Injecting Logic:** The short-term strategy that contains mental game problems while playing and also takes a small step toward resolving them.

2. **Resolution:** The long-term strategy to correct the faulty logic that's causing problems in your mental game.

INJECTING LOGIC

"Injecting logic" is a strategy that builds off of what people and poker players tend to do naturally when facing a mental game problem: talk themselves through it. Of course, sometimes what you say to yourself may as well be throwing gasoline on a grease fire, such as, "I can't believe how f*&%in' unlucky I am!" Other times what you say to yourself can help quite a bit, such as, "It's just variance; I made the right play. Stay calm and just keep playing well." The solution here isn't as simple as just saying the right things to yourself. If it were that simple, you would have already solved your problems.

The only way to fix a mental game problem is by remaining in control of your emotions while you're playing. For example, if you tend to quit or play poorly because of tilt, fixing your tilt problem means at some point you're going to have to take tilt head-on. Injecting logic is the muscle you bring to this fight to delay, reduce, or block out tilt (or other problems) while you're playing. Injecting logic is a necessary bridge to help you achieve resolution and is not a permanent cure. It's a crutch that temporarily contains your mental game problem in the short run, while you work to resolve it in the long run.

Injecting logic works best when:

1. **You catch the build-up of emotion, such as tilt or fear, *before* reaching your emotional threshold.** If not, you have a major uphill battle to regain the ability to think clearly and play well without having to take a break or quit. Why? Once your emotions have crossed the threshold, it becomes harder and harder to think clearly. Injecting logic is really just thinking. Therefore, if your emotions have shut off your ability to think, trying to inject logic is the equivalent of trying to run on a sprained or broken ankle.

2. **Your logic also corrects the underlying flaw.** The fastest way to resolve a mental game problem is by injecting logic that also corrects the underlying flaw that is causing it. Basically, you're working toward two goals at once.

Injecting logic is not the only containment strategy out there. Advice from common poker psychology includes examples of containment strategies, such as taking deep breaths, quitting early, dropping down in stakes, meditating, visualizing, exercising, counting to 10, and telling yourself to calm down. Injecting logic takes them a step further by simultaneously working to resolve the underlying cause. Breathing deeply might help to stop you from going on tilt today, but it won't get to the root of why you tilt in the first place. Only when you resolve the root cause of a mental game issue is it truly solved. A containment strategy that also helps to build toward resolution is more effective and efficient in the long run.

Resolving a mental game issue means that eventually you need to be able to think clearly at times when you typically would not. If you are trying to play without going on tilt, you have to actively fight going on tilt and win that battle. If you are trying to play without fear, you have to fight through your fear and continue to play well. In essence, injecting logic is like using a spotter for the last few reps while lifting weights at the gym—enabling you to steadily build up the strength to control your emotions in a way you couldn't do before.

The six steps below are organized around the strategy of injecting logic. They are purposefully obvious and detailed to make sure those with the toughest mental game problems can make solid progress. Keep in mind that once you get the hang of the first four, you'll be able to do them within just a few seconds.

1. Recognition
2. Deep Breath
3. Injecting Logic

4. Strategic Reminder
5. Repeat as Necessary
6. Quit

1. Recognition

In order to keep an emotional problem from affecting your play, you *must* be able to recognize that it's happening in real time *and* before reaching your threshold. That may seem easy, but it isn't. Poker already gives you enough reasons to delude yourself, so don't make this another one.

If you worked as much on your mental game as you did on your technical skills in poker, recognition would not have to be called out. In poker, this skill is implied; but in the mental game, many players lack the ability to recognize or spot emotional problems before they're already over the edge. Some don't even realize they've been on insane monkey tilt for a few hours until looking up to see 15 buy-ins spewed away.

What you are trying to recognize is the pattern associated with your mental game problem. Fortunately, these problems do not happen randomly. They repeat over and over again, allowing you to learn, for example, your pattern of tilt. Your goal is to know all the signs that indicate you're about to tilt. This gives you a roadmap of your issue, so you can see the signs before driving your game off a cliff.

The better you learn your pattern, the quicker you can recognize it *early*, and the better you can control emotion. Here's how to build the skill of recognition:

A. **Create a profile.** Appendix II includes a questionnaire to help you analyze your mental game. After completing it, dig deeper into the specific problems in your game by writing out, in as much detail as you can, the thoughts, behaviors, actions, emotions, triggers, and poker mistakes that occur with this problem. Ideally, you are also organizing these signs by when they occur, i.e., the first sign when the issue is small, all the way to when it's at its worst.

B. **Study the profile.** Regularly review your profile, especially before playing.

C. **Examine the consequences.** Describe the damage these problems have caused in the past and what they may cause in the future if unresolved. How much does the problem cost? Is it stopping you from moving up in stakes? Does it affect your confidence, life, happiness, or friends and family in any way? Having a clear understanding of the consequences often provides more motivation to take direct and immediate action. Otherwise, it's too easy to keep right on playing thinking nothing bad is about to happen.

D. **Add to the profile.** After sessions, take note of new signs or details about the problem(s).

E. **Set an alarm.** This step is <u>only</u> for players who get so caught up in the action that they don't recognize any mental game problems until after they are finished playing. Set a timer to go off at some regular frequency that isn't too disruptive (i.e. every 30, 45, or 60 minutes). At that time, take a minute to see if the problem is happening, or has recently. If so, quickly detail the thoughts, behaviors, actions, emotions, triggers, and poker mistakes connected to the problem. Yes, this process is disruptive in the short term, but you only have to do it until you build up enough skill to recognize the problem without the timer.

F. **Take action.** Then, as soon as you recognize the signs that your pattern has shown up, go on to step 2.

Additionally, players have found meditation or mindfulness training to be a great tool to build awareness, or recognition, of their pattern.

Even after improving recognition, players still ignore signs that the problem is coming and predictably run into trouble. On the surface, it may seem illogical to ignore these signs when you know what's coming; however, players subconsciously do this just to prove that the problem is that predictable. It's no different from making a play you know is wrong, such as calling a big river bet knowing the villain has the nuts; you need more proof to know you were right.

2. Deep Breath

The primary purpose of a deep breath is to create separation between you and your emotion so you can inject logic. It's similar to leaving the room during a heated argument with someone to clear your head so you can think straight. Taking a few deep breaths while focusing on your breathing can give you just enough separation to stop the problem in its tracks, so you don't have to leave the table.

Depending on your emotional level, you can also use these breaths to either:

Calm Emotion or Increase Intensity

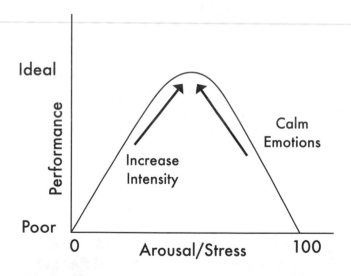

If your emotions are too low—as occurs with motivational problems—use deep breathing to fire you up. If your emotions are too high—as occurs with tilt, anxiety, and confidence problems—use deep breathing to calm you down.

Once you've created separation and either increased or decreased emotion, you're ready to inject logic.

3. Injecting Logic

You're at a disadvantage. You went to a gun fight with a knife. You are fighting against an old pattern, so to turn the table in your favor you need some mental muscle. Injecting logic is it. Thinking is essentially the brain's muscle, so consider injecting logic as a workout to build mental muscle and become stronger.

Basically, the goal of this step is to come up with a phrase or statement to say to yourself (or out loud), which helps to keep your head on straight before you lose it. Ideally, this statement also corrects the faulty logic creating the problem, so you can simultaneously work toward resolution. Many of you already try to think through mental game problems, so consider this just a refining of your technique for better short- and long-term results.

The first way to refine the strategy is to actually write out the statement on a note card, sticky note, word document, cell phone, or whatever you find most convenient. This way, you don't have to rely on a malfunctioning mind to remember it in a critical moment. If you're relying on your memory at this time, you're gambling on the mental game.

The second way to refine the strategy is to have your phrase simultaneously work toward resolution by correcting the flaw or faulty logic causing the problem. (In chapters 5 to 8, specific suggestions for statements are made that correct common faulty logic.) Ultimately, you're looking to create a statement that is in your language, to the point, and *works*! The perfect statement is the one that does the job for you, not the one that sounds best or works for others. Here are a few examples:

- "Bad players have to win; it's just variance. Keep playing well and stay in control." = **Bad Beat**

- "Today I have to weather variance and try to lose the least amount." = **Running Bad**
- "It feels like I can take on anyone, but I can't. Thinking that way is an illusion." = **Overconfidence**

If injecting logic doesn't work, usually it's because:

- Your level of emotion was too strong and already past the threshold.
- Your statement wasn't strong enough.
- Something new threw you off, such as a new mental game issue.
- Accumulated emotion instantly flooded your mind, so you didn't even have a chance to use it.
- Using a voice recording of your statement is a better option for you.

4. Strategic Reminder

Depending on when you catch the problem, your mind may need some time to recover before you're back playing well and into the flow of the game. You can shorten this lag by quickly reminding yourself of a few technical keys to your poker game.

This step has nothing to do with the mental game; this is pure poker strategy.

For example, when fighting the onset of tilt, or actual tilting, you might make errors such as getting too loose pre-flop, ignoring position at the table, forgetting to put opponents on ranges, or not thinking about how your range looks to your opponent. Since you're confronting a malfunctioning mind, the skills that are currently being learned start to disappear from your mind. To keep that from happening, write down either of the following in the same place as your injecting logic statement:

A. A list of <u>only</u> what goes missing from your thought process when making a poker decision.

B. A list of <u>all</u> the factors you consider when making a poker decision.

You can't expect to just play well all of the time. Thinking that way ignores the reality of how the brain functions when your level of emotion rises too high. If you want to play well at times when emotions start to affect your game, you have to work to stay in control. The strategic reminder makes it easier to maintain control of your game.

5. Repeat as Necessary

Your mental game problem is not resolved yet. While you're playing, it's going to keep coming back like a fly that won't leave you alone. Be prepared to go through the first four steps again and again, in order to control your emotions and continue playing well. On some days you'll need to repeat these steps more than on other days.

6. Quitting

Quitting is a skill. Part of that skill is knowing when a mental game issue is too severe to carry on playing and you need to quit. There isn't a hard-and-fast rule for determining when the best time is to quit; sometimes you need to push yourself and play through, while other times you need to quit before it gets too bad. Ultimately, resolving your mental game problems requires that you find a way to play through the problem.

Some players don't have an option; they *have* to find a way to play through problems. Tournament players are the obvious ones, but even cash game professionals making a living from poker need to get in enough hours. The point is simply that without a clear plan to resolve mental game issues, quitting just makes you better at quitting. It doesn't improve issues such as tilt. In fact, some poker players say they don't have a tilt problem because they quit before they tilt. That player still has a tilt problem. Avoiding tilt doesn't mean the issue is gone. Tilt is just not showing up because they aren't playing, but it's still costing them money from lost hours at the table.

With a clear plan to resolve your mental game problems, quitting becomes more strategic. You have options, and every player needs to decide what makes the most sense for them. The key factor to consider is whether or not you can recover and get back to playing well. If the answer is a firm "no," you need to quit and come back later. If the answer is "yes" or "unsure," consider the following way to approach the situation for a greater chance of success:

Playing well during tough times requires your mental strength or muscle to control your emotions. Emotional control is not something you just can expect to happen automatically. Building the mental muscle to do it takes effort, just as lifting weights is required to develop real muscles. In keeping with this comparison, you can view the development of mental muscle the same way as working out in the gym: Start with the amount of weight you can lift and then steadily increase it. Rather than just expecting yourself to continue playing at a time when you typically would quit, push yourself harder to play well and avoid big mistakes for just 5 or 10 more minutes. Then, as you get mentally stronger, add another 5 to 10 minutes. Sure, 5 to 10 minutes can seem minimal, but so would the amount of weight you'd be able to lift on your first trip to the gym. Start small, and then by successfully pushing your sessions longer, session after session, eventually you'll be able to control your emotions for hours, even during some very difficult times.

This strategy is risky of course, but you're a poker player. Evaluate the relative risk/reward for quitting or playing through, and make the best choice depending on the situation.

RESOLUTION

Resolution is the solution to mental game problems. When you train the correction(s) to the flaw(s) causing your mental game problems to the level of Unconscious Competence, you have the right mindset to play poker. The right mindset becomes automatic, like poker skills are when trained to that degree. So even under intense emotional pressure from a terrible run or playing a big pot after just moving up in stakes, you'll stay in the right frame of mind with little effort.

Resolution means the emotion connected to your mental game problem goes away. That means you no longer need to think about handling a bad beat better, you automatically handle it better because a bad beat doesn't trigger anger. By resolving your mental game problems, you'll play better, make more money, and have greater opportunities in poker. Here are two other benefits:

1. **Freeing up mental space increases focus.** Severe mental game issues take a lot of your focus away, even when they aren't present. These problems are similar to a computer program that's running in the background of your computer, but not open on the desktop. These issues are hidden resource hogs that leave you with less mental energy to focus on playing quality poker. You only have so much energy or focus to use at one time. Resolution frees some of it up so you can use it to focus on the action even more, which means you can play at a higher level, longer, and across more tables.

2. **As inchworm illustrates, your best becomes even better.** Most of the elite players in poker have eliminated most mental game issues such as tilt, which means they can continually improve their poker games even more.

Conceptually, resolution may not make sense yet, but it's something you've done already; you just don't realize it. A simple example of this can help make it clear:

> *Let's say you're pissed off at a friend who was an ass the last time you hung out. And let's say you see him several times a week, but don't say anything about being angry for a month. In that time, the anger builds, and there's clearly tension between the two of you. It doesn't stop you from having fun together, but it's not the same as it was before.*
>
> *After a month, you finally say something. He barely remembers, gets defensive, and denies that it could ever happen. The conversation gets heated and you decide to take a break to get your heads on straight (essentially injecting logic). You come back, get an apology, work things out, and agree not to let stuff like that go unsaid for so long.*
>
> *If the problem is truly resolved, any anger between you doesn't just go away in that moment—it never shows up for that reason again.*

Resolution is essentially the same when you do it for your own issues; it's simply the process that differs. Once resolution happens, a bad beat, mistake, or a big pot doesn't trigger emotion. Injecting logic—or any other containment strategy—is no longer needed because there is no emotion to contain. The trigger is still there, but now it is inactive.

Resolution is not a quick fix for most problems. It takes experience, repetition, and focus to replace an old habit and have the new one happen automatically. Players are often fooled into thinking they resolved a problem, but under pressure they revert back to their old ways. That's to be expected. It's really hard to know when a problem has been solved for good. Each time your mental game takes a step backwards, it's an opportunity for you to prove what has been learned to the level of Unconscious Competence and identify what still needs more work.

To work toward resolution in the long term, add the following strategies to what you're doing to contain the problems in the short term.

Mental Hand History

Common approaches to mental game issues tend to look only at a problem and then jump straight to the solution without understanding why it happens. Without understanding why the problem was there to begin with, there's no way to develop a solution that sticks. Instead, you have a surface-level understanding that won't solve the real problem because it has never been identified.

To solve a mental game problem permanently, you need to get to the root of the issue, understand the logical reason it happens, and find out why that logic is flawed. Only when you get to that point can you say that you understand the problem well enough to prescribe a solution that isn't random, nor a placebo.

To make the process of dissecting problems easier, use the 5-step protocol, or the "mental hand history," described below. This protocol is also called the mental hand history because clients send completed versions to me for review, in much the same way they send hand histories to a poker coach. Since you won't have the benefit of direct feedback, each issue is discussed in great detail, allowing you to identify the root cause and correct it yourself.

Be sure to write down your answers, otherwise you'll have too much going on in your mind to get deep enough into the flawed logic to come up with a solid solution. Also, your answers to each step can be as simple as one sentence or several detailed paragraphs. Players vary, so do what makes sense for you. In general, the more detailed your answers, the better.

1. Describe the problem. To begin, write down what you would say if you were describing the problem in your mental game to me. It might

CORRECTING FLAWS IN POKER

Many clients also use this protocol to break down and correct technical flaws in their game. Learning is learning, and the following steps make it easier to *unlearn* an old habit and train a new one.

be something such as, "I go on tilt when a fish sucks-out on me in a big pot" or "I play too loose when I am winning big."

2. Why does it make logical sense that you would react, think, or feel that way? This question may be counterintuitive if the problem in step 1 seems completely illogical or irrational. It's not. Mental game problems always happen for logical reasons and they often have several parts or layers like an onion. If you identify more than one reason while completing this step, follow the next three steps for each reason.

In keeping with the examples above, the logical reason you go on tilt when a fish sucks-out on you is because you always expect to win against bad players; and the reason you loosen up when winning big is because in that moment your confidence is high, poker seems easy, and it feels as if whatever you do, you'll win. The rationale behind these reasons does make sense, but you still need to try and eliminate them.

3. Why is that logic flawed? Avoid using stock answers for why the logic or reason you found in step 2 is flawed, unless you're sure it's correct. Accuracy is critical. Plus, since there are often multiple reasons why your logic is flawed, don't assume that you know all of them. The information in each chapter of this book will help.

Negative emotion happens for predictable reasons and is never the flaw.

In the examples from step 1, the most obvious flaw in your logic is that you're ignoring the realities of poker. No one is capable of always winning against fish or winning no matter how they play. In essence, you believe at a deeper level that you are more in control of the outcome than you actually are. For some, having that level of control is a fantasy they wish could come true. When this wish is proven to not be realistic, you'll react with intense anger—or when it feels as if it has come true, you'll react with intense overconfidence. This illusion of control is an example of a flaw that is not obvious. Fail to correct it and resolution won't happen. *For more on the illusion of control, go to page 216.*

4. What is the correct way to handle the situation? Taking into account steps 2 and 3, this step defines the straightforward correction to the underlying flaw or cause of your mental game problems. Be sure to use affirmative language in at least some part of your answer.

In these examples, if you had skipped steps 2 and 3, the solution you would have come up with might be something like, "Bad beats happen; just don't let them bother you," or "You're probably running hot; don't worry how much you're up." These are pretty good answers that address the flaw in your reaction to variance, but miss the exaggerated sense of control. So, add a statement that corrects the illusion of control, such as, "I can't control the cards, I can only control how well I play and how well I react" or "Playing too loose when I'm up means I've lost control of my game."

5. Why is that correction correct? This question identifies the rationale behind why the answer to step 4 is correct. In some cases, this step can be a bit redundant; but at a minimum, the repetition helps you learn, and it can also add additional clarity or details to the solution.

In these examples, "Control in poker comes through my decisions and how I handle what happens at the table. Bad beats have to happen in the long run for me to be profitable, because without them, the game would fundamentally change." Or "If I loosen up because I'm winning, it means that I believe I'm just going to continue winning in the future no matter what I do. Because of variance, that obviously isn't true, so I just have to force myself to keep playing well and not think I suddenly own poker."

Lastly, achieving resolution means you have learned the correct logic in steps 4 and 5 to the level of Unconscious Competence. To get to that level use the process model, injecting logic, the additional strategies in this chapter, and whatever else you find that works. For the process model, you can turn steps 3, 4, or 5 into a mental game goal to use before you play. For example, "I am going to recognize why the fish winning in the short term is good for me in the long term" or "I am going to maintain a solid strategy whether I am winning or losing." For injecting logic, you can also use what you write in steps 3, 4, and 5 for your statement.

Also keep in mind that as you gather more details about the problem, over time you may need to go through these steps again.

THE MENTAL SIDE OF POKER MISTAKES

Intense emotions block learning and prevent basic skills from getting trained to the level of Unconscious Competence. As a result, players can make exceptionally bad plays when they are on tilt. These are the kind of plays that are so wildly out of line that they've been coined the "Mike Matusow Blow Up," where an otherwise highly skilled player suddenly does something incredibly fishy when they are steaming.

When the emotions connected to a mental game problem block learning, they create a wide range in a player's game. Resolving the problem removes the emotion, and thus the blockage, and their game rapidly improves.

ADDITIONAL STRATEGIES

Tracking Improvement
There is no such thing as Hold'em Manager or PokerTracker for the mental game (yet). For now, if you want to be more objective in knowing how you're progressing in the mental game, you need to keep track of your progress in some way other than keeping all the information in your head.

Tracking your mental game is important because improvement is often subtle. If you miss it, your motivation to keep working drops from falsely believing that you're not improving. When you recognize that you're improving, you can gain confidence; conversely, if you realize that you are not improving, your strategy will be easier to adjust because you will have actual data to use.

Here are some ways to know your mental game problems are improving:

- You have increased recognition of your patterns in real time at the table.
- You can recognize the signs of your patterns before reaching your threshold. (That doesn't mean you can control your emotions yet, just that you better recognize what's happening.)
- You have a stronger ability to control emotion while playing.
- You make fewer poker mistakes.
- You have a stronger ability to play longer while battling a problem.
- You quit faster (for the right reasons).
- You're able to recover a solid mindset faster.
- The urge to berate your opponents lessens.
- You have fewer negative thoughts.
- You feel normal faster after a bad session.
- Your absolute worst is better than it was before.
- You recognize new layers of the problem, or entirely new problems.
- You have an increased desire to work on your game after the session.

Writing

Writing can be a powerful tool to help you work through all aspects of your mental game. That does not mean you have to be a writer. It's a simple, free tool that:

- Builds recognition.

- Speeds learning.

- Takes what is in your head and makes it more concrete.

- Creates a record for you to refer back to in the future for comparison or reference.

- Frees up your mind, so you don't have to remember as much.

- Organizes issues, so you're more prepared to take them head-on.

- Releases emotion and captures data to help you break down the problem in the future.

- Helps to keep your game organized today; and if your game ever falls apart, it's easier to put it back together again in the future.

Often, the hardest thing for players when they begin writing is knowing what to write about. There are suggestions in each chapter of this book, but if you'd like to get started right away, answer the questions in Appendix II.

Accumulated Emotion

When emotions have built up over long periods of time, the intensity of the emotion can be so strong that it instantly overwhelms your mind and ability to remain in control.

When you're nervous in a big pot, you're experiencing the actual anxiety felt that day plus the old anxiety that's been felt in many big pots before. Emotion accumulates and that's why you fly off the handle five hands into your session after taking a sick beat. You say to yourself, "Why the f*#@ does this always happen to me?" because you're pissed off about the beat you just took and the ones that *always* happen. Emotion from all of those bad beats accumulates in your memory, and collectively they instantly overwhelm your mind.

Breaking down accumulated emotion requires more work away from the table because injecting logic won't work. The emotion is so intense that it quickly overwhelms your ability to think, and thus your ability to remain in control. The mind is only so powerful. The way to control emotion is by resolving the old emotion. When there is less emotion to contain you then have a better chance of staying in control. The steps below can help you to resolve old emotion.

1. **Realize that accumulated emotion is a real risk each time you play—so take it seriously for a while.** Don't expect it to disappear quickly. Instead, look to steadily decrease the intensity of the emotion you feel, while increasing your ability to control your emotion. That process isn't like a light switch. Some days will be easier than others because of the range that exists in your ability to control emotion.

2. **Do a mental hand history for each issue.** Then study what you've written as you would a poker concept you were having trouble learning.

3. **Work hard to build recognition of your pattern.** Then while playing, work hard to recognize it sooner and sooner.

4. **Set an alarm.** See page 53.

5. **Rewrite the past.** Not literally, since that's impossible. Instead, do a mental hand history for any old memories that stand out around this issue, treating the memory as if it just happened.

6. **Write about what you learned from these old memories.** Even negative experiences are often positive because of what they teach you not to do. Taking what you've learned in the past and using it to make you stronger today, goes a long way in resolving old emotion.

7. **If you're critical of your past failures, errors, or the like, see *page 118*.**

8. **Remove any expectations that this shouldn't be happening or should have already been fixed.** If that were true, you wouldn't be in this position. There are many players in the same position, so don't wallow in the fact that you have to deal with it and just do what's necessary to fix it.

9. **Address the subtle pieces of the problem.** Use the mental hand history to help you to identify and resolve previously unknown pieces of the problem.

10. **Even though the issues may be different, consider using any of the steps for fixing desperation tilt on *page 148*.**

Accumulated emotion is the most difficult problem in the mental game to fix, and doing it on your own is going to be a challenge. If you find the instructions here too difficult to follow, or they aren't working well enough, consider consulting a psychologist or therapist. When resolving emotion is especially tough, there may be a connection to a problem outside of poker that's getting in the way, which is another reason to consider working with a professional.

Conclusion

With the right strategy, problems in your mental game become opportunities to improve as a player. Trying to block out emotional problems in today's game only takes you so far. If you have higher aspirations in poker, are trying to establish yourself as a winning player, or are a regular looking to stay ahead, resolving mental game problems is how you can stop beating yourself and start beating other players.

5

TILT

Tilt = Anger + Bad Play

THE DEFINITION OF TILT as defined by conventional poker wisdom is too broad. Sometimes tilt just means playing badly; but it also can mean playing badly because of winning, or playing too loose, conservatively, or drunk. Tilt is hard to eliminate because the definition is so broad, it basically includes everything except playing great poker.

To fix tilt you have to know why you played badly. Only when you know the cause of your poor play can you devise a specific strategy to fix it. A strategy can only be as specific as the problem is defined. There are hundreds of things that cause you to play poorly, and the solution for each one requires a unique strategy. If you think being specific isn't that important, consider the following comparison.

You might hear something along the lines of this from a player:

> *"I was doing fine, making some good reads and was up a buy-in; then I went on tilt and spewed off all my chips."*

71

In general, poker players don't analyze tilt in the same way they would a poker hand. Instead, their analysis of tilt is the mental game equivalent of analyzing a hand like this:

> "I'm in the small blind, it's folded to the cut off who raises to $10, I have ace-queen suited, then I make a technical mistake and lose my stack."

You may as well say, "I sat down at the table, yada yada yada, I lost." All the relevant information you need to analyze the hand properly and find out why you lost a stack is left out. Without that information, there's no way to actually improve your poker skill. Tilt is no different.

Spend enough time observing poker players and it becomes clear that the majority of references to tilt refer to players being frustrated, angry, or enraged. It's for that reason this book defines tilt as an anger issue. That doesn't mean the solution is to just not be angry. Thinking you can permanently flick tilt off like a switch is a fantasy. Plus, you're assuming anger is the problem. Anger is the symptom—not the real problem.

As discussed in chapter 4, solving your tilt problem means both successfully managing tilt at the table while also working away from the table to resolve the cause of it. Both sides of the strategy are essential, so avoid falling into the trap of believing that strategies such as taking deep breaths, taking breaks, quitting, going to the gym, holding your breath, or positive thinking are permanent solutions. These strategies are best used to manage tilt until resolution eliminates it.

The goal of this chapter is to provide the background information you need to take tilt head-on and eliminate it from your game. Organized in successive sections, the information about tilt steadily becomes more detailed and specific. While the details at times may seem like overkill, mastery is all about the small details—just ask any high-stakes pro.

The Nature of Anger

Anger is the emotion that represents conflict. Conflict at a basic level is a disagreement. Conflict is most obvious when it's between you and someone else, as happens when a car cuts you off, a friend acts like a drunken idiot, or someone berates you at the poker table for making a bad call. Anger is not inherently a bad thing. It can be an incredible motivator to take action, but it can also lead to major problems. The first key to solving your tilt problem is to understand the specific cause of your anger.

Conflict between you and poker, and you and other poker players, is much easier to notice than conflict between you and yourself—though not in a multiple personality disorder *Me, Myself and Irene*[1] sort of way. Players often describe feeling as if they are "fighting with themselves" trying to control tilt. This conflict is not made up. It's real and exists between what a player knows consciously and the flaws that exist in their Unconscious Competence. Essentially, they are fighting to keep these flaws from causing tilt.

There are times when you're able to win the fight and keep the beast in its cage; other times your conscious mind is overwhelmed by the intensity of your anger and you lose control. Losing control is often hard to wrap your mind around because logically you know how you *should* be thinking and why tilt is irrational, so why isn't that enough? These are the three possibilities:

1. You have the correct logic and need to learn it to the level of Unconscious Competence.

2. Accumulated tilt rapidly overwhelms your mental defenses.

3. You think you have all the pieces of the logic puzzle to resolve the problem, but you actually don't.

The vast majority of poker players relate best to the third answer, and the purpose of this chapter is to give you those missing pieces.

---

1   A 2000 Farrelly Brothers comedy starring Jim Carrey as a cop with a split personality.

Accumulated Tilt

The anger that causes tilt is not just the result of one particular session or tournament; it can accumulate over time. When anger goes unresolved, it is carried over into the future. If you've ever insta-tilted as if a bomb went off, it's because of accumulated tilt. Most commonly this happens during prolonged runs of bad variance. Each day it gets easier and easier to tilt because the anger from the day before carries over, much like a cup that's steadily filling up with water. Each day some, but not all of the water gets poured out; so the next time water goes in, it's already at a higher level and needs less to overflow. In poker, you're able to work through some of the anger that accumulates from playing, but if it's not enough to reset your mind completely, you'll reach your threshold faster the next time you play.

As they relate to emotional control, your thoughts are less powerful than your emotions themselves. No matter how mentally tough you are, accumulated tilt can overpower your ability to remain in control of your emotions. This means that the only way to deal with accumulated tilt is by working through your emotions away from the table. *Use the strategy on page 66, as well as the general strategy outlined later in this chapter, to resolve accumulated tilt.*

The Tilt of Tilt

Anger is created in two places. The most significant form of anger comes from bad habits learned at the level of Unconscious Competence. For example, you hate losing and then get angry when you do; you believe you deserve to win because you're a better player and get angry when a fish sucks-out; or you can't stand bad drivers and lose your mind after getting cut off.

Anger is also created by recognizing that you're angry: "the tilt of tilt". Essentially, you're angry because you're angry—being pissed off because a mistake pisses you off, tilting because you let an opponent tilt you, or tilting because you have no idea how to fix your tilt problem.

These extra layers of mental anger are basically like adding another log onto a bonfire. While flawed logic in the Unconscious Competence started the fire, using your mind more efficiently is necessary to solve your tilt problem. The previous three chapters make it simpler for you to think through tilt. So simple, in fact, you might get tilted that you didn't figure it out before. Players often don't even realize that they're adding fuel; they think it's water.

The Benefit of Tilt

You read that right. Tilt can be a good thing. It can be used to improve your game. Of course, the ultimate goal is not to tilt at all, but since you can't just wish the problem away, it's better to use tilt to make you a better player.

As discussed in chapter 3, when any emotion (in this case, anger) becomes more intense, it has a profound impact on the thinking part of your brain, eventually shutting it down completely. Thinking provides protection against flaws in your game that have not been corrected at the level of Unconscious Competence. Since it's tough to know when poker skills have reached Unconscious Competence (since it's unconscious), tilt gives you a perfect window into that part of your game. Reality can be harsh when you see how little of your game is actually mastered. However, in a game where success and profitability depend on accurate assessments of your game, tilt can be a good thing.

When you go on tilt, it's easy to focus just on how badly you played. But you need to recognize that not everything goes to hell, you still do some things very well. If you still throw away marginal hands out of position, it means you've mastered the importance of position and good hand selection. Even though you might be playing too loose or tight while tilting, you may also be bet sizing well, or thin value betting in the right spots.

Of course, there's the obvious flip side where a bad beat or constant aggression sends you over the edge and your greatest weaknesses show up. All of a sudden you may find yourself in no man's land trying to bluff a donkey who clearly has a hand, demonstrating that perhaps you still don't automatically know when to take your foot off the gas in a pot. If you find yourself calling too loose or chasing draws without the right odds, this could demonstrate a lack of deep understanding of the mathematical side of the game, or it could highlight an inner urge to gamble.

Although the mistakes that you make when on tilt are often basic, they can only happen because you have not mastered the correction. Anger plays a role for sure; if you didn't become so angry, you'd be able to think as usual and avoid these mistakes. Nonetheless, the flaws in your poker skill need to be fixed, and tilt helps you to identify them. *For more on how to use tilt to improve your play, go to page 150.*

Winner's Tilt

Playing badly after winning a lot is not caused by anger. The mistakes made when winning are most often caused by positive emotions, and to a lesser degree the fear of losing money back. Winner's tilt is caused by overconfidence shutting down the thinking part of the brain. Confidence is an emotion and too much of it produces mistakes for the same reason as anger. However, the underlying cause of anger is different than the cause of overconfidence and thus requires a different strategy to solve it. Go to chapter 8 for more.

Tilt Profile

Despite many commonalities, every player tilts in slightly different ways and for different reasons. One of the best times to understand your tilt better is immediately after a session where you tilted, because it's so fresh in your mind. Of course, since tilt is so costly, your best bet is to spend time thinking about previous situations where you've tilted. Use the questions on the next page as a guide to begin analyzing and identifying the details of your tilt. If specifics are hard to find, that's fine; everyone has a different starting point.

- What causes you to tilt? (Bad beats, losing to fish, running bad, etc.)
- What are the things you say to yourself out loud, or to other players, when frustration starts rising and when tilted?
- How do you know that you're on tilt? What's the first thing you notice?
- How does your body react to tilt? (Head gets hot, body is sweaty, heart races, fist is clenched, etc.)
- Can you identify the point when tilt starts shutting down your thinking?
- At what point do you take action to deal with tilt?

The answers to these questions, and whatever else comes to mind about tilt, form the baseline of your tilt profile. It is impossible to control something you don't understand, so the goal at this point is to continue building your tilt knowledge base. While accuracy matters a lot when it comes to resolving tilt, simply increasing your knowledge often leads to at least some improvement. That may not mean you can control it at all times, but since increased knowledge or recognition is often the first of many small steps, you're off to a solid start.

THINK YOU DON'T TILT?

There are players who believe they don't tilt because they quit before they do. Does this mean they don't tilt? According to the formula at the beginning of this chapter, technically yes, since they aren't making mistakes. On the other hand, there's clearly an anger problem that hasn't been resolved and is being managed by quitting. Often, these players develop motivational problems because they aren't getting in enough volume and eventually forget that tilt was the cause. Basically, they learn to live with the elephant in the room so well, they eventually forget it's there.

Having a baseline for your tilt problems is also important because it gives you a solid point of reference to evaluate progress in the future. Tracking your mental game is not like tracking poker stats. There are times when the intensity of your anger feels the same as before, but in reality, your mistakes aren't as bad, you recognize tilt faster, you take action against tilt earlier, you quit a session sooner, and the thoughts in your head are less negative. *For more about tracking improvement, go to page 64.*

For many players, small improvements have to happen before they can take full control of tilt. A tilt profile that's written out gives them the ability to see the small improvements that are normally hard to see. It's critical to recognize these small improvements so they avoid falsely abandoning a strategy that is working in slower or less significant ways than they would expect.

Seven Types of Tilt

The following list briefly describes the most common types of tilt:

- **Running Bad Tilt:** The tilt that's caused by a run of bad cards is not actually a unique type of tilt. Instead, one (or more) of the other types of tilt happens so frequently in such a short amount of time that your mind can't reset itself before the next time you play. As a result, tilt builds up and hangs over your head like a dark cloud.

- **Injustice Tilt:** Bad beats, coolers, and suck-outs are prime examples of triggers that make you feel cursed and make poker feel unfair.

- **Hate-losing Tilt:** Many players hate losing even though they realize how much variance impacts results in the short run. Wanting to win is not the problem—the problem is how you handle the inevitable losses.

- **Mistake Tilt:** Making mistakes is frustrating for many logical reasons; these reasons just happen to be flawed because of inaccurate views about learning.

- **Entitlement Tilt:** Classic Phil Hellmuth tilt is caused by believing that you deserve to win for X, Y, or Z reason. Winning is a possession and you tilt when someone undeserving takes it from you.

- **Revenge Tilt:** Disrespect, constant aggressive action, and opponents thinking they're better than you are just a few of the reasons why you seek vengeance at the table.

- **Desperation Tilt:** The urge to win your money back and get unstuck is so strong, it makes you play monster sessions, force the action, and jump up in stakes.

Greater detail about each type of tilt is provided in the corresponding sections within this chapter. How you choose to read this chapter is entirely up to you. It may make sense to jump to whichever section fits your tilt profile the best. Although, there are many reasons to read all of the following tilt sections. One main reason is that you may recognize tendencies and triggers in a type of tilt you wouldn't have immediately associated with your game.

BARRY'S TAKE

Understanding Your Opponents' Tilt

Another reason to familiarize yourself with all the types of tilt is to better understand your opponents' tilt. Although this book does not profess to be a traditional poker strategy book, understanding common mental game flaws and patterns adds another way to analyze your opponents. You wouldn't want the players at your table seeing a copy of your tilt profile because they could use it to exploit you. Having a greater understanding of another player's mental game leaks can help you create an edge where few people can claim to have one.

General Strategy for Tilt

Building from the general model laid out in chapter 4, the following strategy applies to all types of tilt. Within each section are specific strategies to help you break down each specific type of tilt even more.

1. **Recognition:** It's not enough to just be familiar with your pattern of tilt when you're away from the table. You have to be able to clearly recognize the signs that you're on tilt or heading that way in the actual moment; otherwise, you can't gain control of it. For some players, these signs are too small and weak to stop them from tilting. Study your tilt profile as you would a poker concept, and build the skill of recognition. Only when you can recognize the signs that you're tilting *while playing*, can you control it.

2. **Preparation:** Before each time you play poker, review your tilt profile, injecting logic statement(s), strategic reminders, and any other parts of your strategy so they're in the front of your mind. That way, you'll be more likely to spot the early signs of tilt, and thus more likely to take action before anger reaches your emotional threshold and begins to shut down your ability to think.

3. **Performance:** Make controlling tilt a priority. Keep an eye out for the signs of tilt and inject logic when you notice them. Also, mark or make a note of hands where frustration or anger shows up. That way you can easily gather more details about tilt after the session.

4. **Evaluation:** What you do after a session or tournament depends on the severity of your tilt.

   On a day when tilt is mild, focus your evaluation on the improvements you made with tilt. Pay attention to spots that previously would have tilted you, where instead you were able to remain in control. Analyze what you did to successfully manage tilt, and take note of any new signs. Review your mental hand history to reinforce the correction.

On days when tilt is significant, but not horrible, take notes soon after you're done playing. While the details of your tilt are still fresh in your mind, add any new details to your tilt profile about what pissed you off, the mistakes you made, or the signs that you were on tilt. Don't assume the details are always the same as the other times you tilted; look for differences. At a minimum, if the details are the same, paying more attention to them increases the skill of recognition. Basically, you're writing step 1 of the mental hand history, and that alone can reduce anger. If you're objective enough after finishing step 1, you'll speed up the process of resolution by going through the remaining four steps.

When tilt is really bad, even though it may be the last thing that you *want* to do, taking notes can help you deal with tilt better in the future. Spew out what's in your head by productively venting. Yes, venting is a great thing, but players often do it solely to other players who don't want to hear it. Instead, by writing (or venting to a friend first and then writing), you get the critical details about the cause of your tilt out of your head to a place where you can see them. Often players ignore these gold nuggets of insight because they don't even realize how valuable they are for solving tilt. By capturing them, you have the critical data to help you decode the cause of your tilt.

Productive venting also allows your brain to relax, and players who do it regularly say that it helps them feel normal faster. Complete the remaining four steps of the mental hand history within the next few days.

CLIENT'S STORY

Liz "RikJamesB1atch" Herrera
Heads Up NL up to $50/$100

"I was pretty much your average grinder before I talked with Jared back in 2008. I had a decent win rate of 3bb/100 playing 6 max NL multi tables, and was winning 5bb/100 playing Heads Up. When I played online, I kept my gender secret because I wasn't interested in fame; I just wanted to be respected. That's where my poker name came from; it was such a macho name that nobody would ever think I was female (it's funny, because I hear Phil Galfond chose "OMGClayAiken" so players would think he was a woman).

The reason I wanted to talk with Jared was that I was tilting much more at Heads Up. Poker can be downright infuriating sometimes, and it makes you want to slam the hell out of your mouse. I always thought tilt was normal. I had a conversation with a respected 2+2 poster and coach who actually told me tilt was just part of the game. I would tilt two to three times in a session, and assumed that I just had to deal with it . . . until I read Jared's thread on Stoxpoker and decided to give him a try.

Right away he helped me to see how many types of tilt there are. He taught me how to identify them and got me to write down my own personal tilt triggers to determine what I would do and why I would do it. I would keep them written on a note card and focus on it while I was playing. When one of those triggers would show up, I'd remind myself that there was potential I might go on tilt; so I would do breathing exercises and stop and think for a minute.

He also made me think about my signs of tilt—the things I would do when I was on tilt, like being overly aggressive, acting without thinking, and making bad bluffs. When I noticed these showing up, I definitely knew it was time to take a break. After doing this for several weeks, I eventually got to the point where I didn't even need to take a break; I could just take some deep breaths and just keep on playing—the fact that I had noticed them was enough to stop me from tilting.

Really the thing that helped me the most was the concept of the journal. When he first mentioned it, I thought it was lame and I didn't want to do it. I just had an image of a teenager writing in a diary about her feelings. Six months after fighting him on it, I gave it a shot and wow, was I blown away and upset I hadn't done it much sooner. It helped me really understand what I needed to do. It created a map, in a sense, which really accelerated my learning process. Now I have a journal for just about everything I do and it's such a helpful tool. I use it for tracking, but also to explore new ideas and break down my mistakes in a somewhat positive manner.

The results of my work with Jared didn't happen overnight; it took a few months to really put them into play. Half the work is the advice he gives; the other half is up to you. Using what he gave me had a huge effect on my win rate. Even including those old hands, my win rate now is almost 12bb/100 over a million hands from $2/$4 all the way to $50/$100 Heads Up."

What Progress Looks Like and How to Keep it Going

The first step when making progress is very often just better recognition of tilt as it happens. That doesn't mean you can control it yet; but better recognition is a *critical* first step to being able to gain control. Tilt is a complex puzzle that requires continual attention to its many pieces.

Here are some other key markers to look for when evaluating progress:

- You spot the signs of tilt earlier and can remain in control more easily.
- You recover, or feel normal, faster after terrible sessions.
- It takes more tilt-inducing stuff to reach your threshold.

- It's easier to push through tilt and play longer.
- You're able to refocus and get back to playing well faster.
- The intensity of your anger is lower.
- Your greatest poker weaknesses have improved.

It's also critical that you catalog improvements in the worst aspects of your tilt. If you are making progress, you have solid data to reference in your tilt profile. Emotions are so fluid that, without having a written record, it can seem as though nothing has improved, when in fact, many aspects of your tilt have. Too often players don't realize they are making progress and quit doing what was working. By seeing these small improvements, you'll gain confidence and extra motivation to keep working on your tilt. Plus, if you aren't improving, at least you have proof, and can use the data you've gathered to make adjustments to your strategy.

It is also important to remember that when making progress there are often times when you take a few steps backwards. While they can be demoralizing, these are great opportunities to better understand the cause(s) of your tilt, so you're better prepared to prevent these missteps in the future. Since one definition of being crazy is doing the same thing time and time again while expecting different results, try using all that tilt gives you rather than just hoping it goes away.

RUNNING BAD TILT

Going on tilt when running bad is so common that players often think of it as an actual part of the game. While there are few things worse in poker than sustained periods of bad luck, there are few things better at helping you identify mental and technical flaws in your game. (In a twisted sort of way, having a bad run of cards is actually a form of good variance.)

Running bad tilt is caused by a form of accumulated tilt that develops over days, weeks, months, or years of bad cards. It's a vicious cycle that builds momentum because variance makes you tilt, which makes you play badly, which makes you tilt more, which carries over to the next day, which means you'll probably tilt more quickly. Then when you do tilt again, you tilt harder, so your losses pile up even more, which makes you quit early. Then you tilt because you quit, so it weighs on your mind more and you struggle sleeping. You wake up tired and feel like you have to play, but then you get screwed again . . . play bad . . . tilt again . . . make more mistakes . . . tilt some more . . . play a monster session to get unstuck . . . fall deeper into poker hell . . . think winning is the answer but you can't win . . . tilt more . . . can't stop playing . . . tilt more because you can't stop tilting . . . believe no one has run worse . . . want to quit the game . . . not really you just need to win again.

Sound familiar?

Your pattern likely has differences, since everyone's is a bit unique. However, the commonalities among poker players who tilt when running bad are striking once you dig a bit deeper. The key thing to keep in mind is that while running bad other types of tilt are triggered repeatedly in a short amount of time. If bad beats cause you to tilt, then during periods where you run bad, you'll tilt more because bad beats are happening more often, sometimes in quick succession. Having your aces cracked during a good run doesn't bother you because it doesn't happen that often, plus winning offsets any anger.

A streak of bad variance doesn't cause tilt. It reveals the underlying reasons you tilt. If you aren't sure which of the other types of tilt running bad exposes, your thoughts can help you to implicate them. For example:

- "This isn't fair, I'm due to run normal, I never win a flip!" = **Injustice Tilt**
- "How is it possible to lose like this again!" = **Hate-losing Tilt**
- "I knew that! Dammit, how can I play so bad?!" = **Mistake Tilt**
- "I'm too good of a player for this to happen. How can I keep losing to this donkey?" = **Entitlement Tilt**

- "I'm gonna 3-bet this idiot; who the f*&% does he think he is!? F*&% you I shove." = **Revenge Tilt**
- "I'll stay here for a f*&%ing week if I have to win!" = **Desperation Tilt**

After identifying the type(s) of tilt exposed by running bad, read the corresponding section to help you resolve it. Once the underlying causes of your tilt are corrected, you'll no longer tilt when running bad, no matter how many beats you take. A sustained bad run likely still will be frustrating, but you'll be able to be in control and play well through it.

If you can't isolate any other types of tilt, or if it seems much more like running bad is the real issue, you can take a broader approach. Variance is a difficult concept for players to truly wrap their heads around. While many get it, their knowledge of variance is often absent when their mind is on the edge of disaster. The reality is that knowledge of variance is a skill like any other, so it plays by the same rules. Only what's trained to the level of Unconscious Competence is guaranteed to show up under emotional pressure; everything else isn't mastered yet and needs more work. Despite what you may already know about variance, you need to learn it better. Perhaps that's why players who come from mathematical or financial backgrounds tend to thrive in poker. They already have a bedrock of knowledge on the nature of variance.

Although you can't actually control variance, you can gain greater control of your game by learning more about it. Dig deeper into the subtleties of variance to understand it beyond the obvious coolers, suck-outs, and bad beats. Ideally, strengthening your skill for recognizing variance should be done on a regular basis. Having this skill allows you to know in the moment whether you are running bad, playing badly, or getting outplayed, which ultimately keeps the mind more stable. *For more on the skill of recognizing variance, go to page 211.*

CLIENT'S STORY

Matt "mbolt1" Bolt
$3/$6 to $50/$100 NLHE

DRAGTHEBAR COACH

"Early on, I progressed really quickly having been staked and coached by Dusty Schmidt. Having that opportunity also allowed me to move up in stakes rapidly, so in a few months a bad losing day went from being a couple of hundred bucks to $5,000. I ran pretty well all the way through the stakes; every time I moved up I ran good and immediately crushed. I didn't really have any real experience with negative variance until I settled in to the mid- to high-stakes games.

Now I was subjected to losing days you can't even comprehend when you are 16 tabling $2/$4. The money was never that big of an issue; for me it was losing. I thought it was way worse to lose $5,000 over the course of a week playing $3/$6 than it was to lose $80,000 in a day playing $50/$100.

What Jared did was get me thinking about the right things, and he gave me a better understanding of why my brain did what it did. You naturally develop a tolerance for variance when you play high volume, but our talks sped up the process.

It's so incredibly frustrating when you're running bad. There were times in 2010 I didn't even think I was playing poker, I thought I was playing a game called *You Lose*, where I showed up to the tables every day to lose. In my mind the difference between a great player and a mediocre player is how they deal with bad runs. One thing he said that sticks out was, 'Michael Jordan never made a dime in the weight room.' I like thinking of Jordan working his ass off in the weight room not making any money. That's what the bad run is for me—working hard to lose as little as possible.

It's not easy to do. On the mental side of poker, everything that is important for a successful player is almost the exact opposite of human nature. Nobody wants to quit playing when they are down money; they want to chase their losses, but want to quit real early when they're ahead. When a good poker player is running well, they want to stay on the table; all the conditions are right and they're usually playing their A+ game. When it's bad, they want to quit. Inexperienced players behave the opposite way. In my experience, everything that you instinctively think is right, is wrong in the poker mental game.

I was always bad at doing homework, so for a long time all I did with Jared was our sessions, and not much else. I found that talking with him would help immensely; but after a while without a session, things would start to slide because it wasn't really sinking in. So finally, I started filling out worksheets after my sessions where I evaluated my play, mental state, and also noted how much variance played a part. This really helped me cope with downswings. Everyone naturally remembers all the spots they were unlucky and forgets all the spots they were lucky.

Previously, I would think, 'Wow, I'm the unluckiest person in the world, this is so unfair, I deserve to win more.' I would think it's fine to be unlucky for a few days, as long as I'm lucky after to make up for it. I know that's not rational, but in the moment you feel the massive sense of injustice and frustration that the luck didn't even out. Variance still sucks, but now I don't focus much on how unlucky I am. What's the point? I try to ignore results, and focus on playing each hand as well as possible. I recently had a 90 buy-in downswing and have no doubt that I played during that time because I was tracking it closely the whole way."

INJECTING LOGIC

YOU DON'T CONTROL HOW YOU RUN, SO WHY FOCUS ON IT?

YOU'RE A SHITTY PSYCHIC AND CAN'T PREDICT WHEN IT'S GOING TO TURN AROUND. ALL YOU CAN DO IS KEEP PLAYING WELL.

Focused More on Results than Quality

Poker has evolved rapidly in the last decade. Part of that evolution is more players shifting their focus to the quality of their play, rather than solely on results in the short run. Since it's a new concept to the poker community at large (previously some have been heard uttering they would rather be lucky than good), players often complain that they know focusing only on results is wrong, but can't help it when they are running bad.

Focusing more on the quality of your play is a skill, which means it plays by the rules of the ALM. However, players often incorrectly assume that making a results-oriented action, such as checking the cashier or getting annoyed by a bad beat, means no progress was made towards their focus on quality. Unless you are tracking progress with notes, or have a photographic memory, it's impossible to accurately identify the subtle improvements in this skill. Thus, smaller signs of improvement such as increased recognition, checking results less frequently, having slightly less frustration, being more focused on quality, or reviewing more hands after a session, are often ignored when you're only looking for end results.

Every time you go through a period of running bad, it's an opportunity to prove just how much you have learned. Only when skill consistently shows up under extreme emotional pressure can you prove what has been learned to the level of Unconscious Competence. Everything else is still in the process of being learned.

IT'S ALL SKILL; YOU'RE JUST NOT BEING REWARDED RIGHT NOW.

IF IT'S ALL SKILL IN THE LONG RUN, THEN YOU NEED TO FOCUS ON SKILL IN THE SHORT RUN.

Booking a Win

As a sustained bad run wears on, the desire to lock up a winning session seems more and more like a good option. Bad runs can make it hard to remember what it's like to even win, so you book a win to get back the feeling of winning, make some money, and avoid the pain of another losing session. Booking a win (along with playing at lower stakes or fewer tables) is something that conventional poker wisdom advocates for handling running bad, especially when it is also affecting confidence.

Well, is booking a win the right thing to do? Or should you just keep pressing on, knowing that as long as you're playing well, eventually it'll turn around?

The answer is: It depends. Your job as a player is to evaluate risk. Here are two things to consider when making your decision:

1. **Booking a win is a great option when your confidence is low and it's obvious that you are playing poorly.** If you feel crushed and can't remember the last time you won at the tables, book the win. With your edge so low, and perhaps even -EV when on tilt, continuing to play is poker suicide. If booking a win can boost your confidence a bit and get you on the road to playing better, then do it. Just realize that booking a win does not solve your confidence problems; it's a temporary fix to problems that, if not addressed directly, will show back up the next time you run bad. Rather than having your confidence constantly go up and down alongside your results, read chapter 8 and start trying to develop stable confidence.

2. **Play a little longer if you've improved your tilt problem and proven you can control it.** Pushing yourself to play slightly longer—even just 10 minutes—builds mental muscle, strengthens poker skills, increases confidence, and works to resolve the underlying cause of your tilt.

Poker/Life Balance

As the bad run wears on, the effects can start to bleed into your personal life. Poker becomes tougher to put out of your mind, losses affect your mood, you snap at friends, you don't feel like doing much, and it's harder to focus, fall asleep, and enjoy your free time. For some players, it takes just one session before poker starts affecting them personally; for others it takes longer.

The way to keep poker out of your life is by creating a bubble around it. Follow the steps below to help you to put poker down so you can move on with your life. Stopping poker from bleeding into your life requires direct action. Here's a strategy that's helped many players:

Step 1: Vent on paper or the computer. Most people vent unproductively. They do it to other people or to themselves. Instead, do your venting on paper or the computer to get your thoughts about poker out of your head and to create a record of what is pissing you off. Basically, you're trying to create a description of what happened while it's fresh in your mind. You don't need to do anything with this information, you're just getting it out of your head with the intention of analyzing your tilt once you've calmed down and can take a more objective view. If you need to take a short break before you write, that's fine, though it's best if you can come back within a few hours.

Step 2: Take notes on your poker or mental mistakes after the session. You don't need to do a hardcore analysis—just organize the hands and capture some of the game flow so you can work on your weaknesses more accurately in the future. It's easier to do this when you've marked or identified hands during the session.

Step 3: Take a break. At this point you've done all that you can do. There's nothing more that you can do to help your game other than relax and give yourself a break. You can't change what happened, but you can use what happened to better understand the technical or mental problems in your game with an eye on becoming a better player in the future. You've done that in steps 1 and 2. Now your mind needs to relax, allowing it to recover before playing again.

Step 4: Put poker out of your mind, or put your thoughts down on paper. It's possible that thoughts about poker will continue to pop into your mind even after going through the first three steps. If they do, try to force them out of your mind by refocusing on what you're doing. If they persist, then take a few notes down so you can go on with your life.

While thinking about poker right after getting destroyed is rarely what you want to do, it is a great way to stop your mind from grinding on poker at times you'd rather not.

Predicting Bad Beats

A bad run is made worse when your mind starts predicting more losses. You get dealt aces and instantly assume they'll get cracked. Spike middle set on the flop, and of course your opponent's check raise means they have top set. Be a 20-1 favorite going into the river and you know a suckout is coming. It's just a foregone conclusion that you're going to lose, you're just playing to find out how it's going to happen this time.

For some players, the accuracy of their predicting power makes it seem as if bad beats are happening because they're thinking one is coming. This illusion is created by not realizing the mind makes predictions based on recent events.

The mind has the ability to anticipate the future, just as the body does. When your body is moving, it's constantly making predictions so it's prepared. One example where this prediction goes wrong happens when walking up a flight of stairs and not paying attention to how many steps there actually are. If you anticipate a step that isn't there, you'll practically trip because your body's prediction was wrong.

Whether in reference to the body or the mind, a prediction is based solely on the information available at that time. When running bad, the mind is drawing from a pool of data that is heavily skewed towards losing. Naturally your mind predicts more losing. On the flip side, when you're running well, the same thing happens in the other direction: You see nothing but more winning in the future because there's far more recent data to suggest it'll continue.

Predicting more losing is only a problem if:

1. You start playing a losing strategy in a desperate attempt to avoid taking losses.
2. You believe that your predictions are an actuality of what the future holds.

Unless you have real psychic power (why are you reading this book if you do?), believing that your mind is controlling results is an illusion. This illusion of control is subtle, and is an underlying issue that needs to be addressed directly. Resolve it, and predicting bad beats will no longer add an additional layer of anger or affect your decision making when running bad. *For more on the illusion of control, go to page 216.*

 YOU CONTROL HOW YOU RESPOND TO THE CARDS, NOT WHAT CARDS ARE DEALT.

Resetting Your Mind

As a bad run wears on, having to deal with more tilt-inducing stuff (triggers) also wears on your mind. When the frequency of your triggers is typical, your mind can be reset after a good night's sleep, a night out with friends, or a good workout. Unfortunately, when tilt keeps building up day after day, it becomes harder and harder for you to show up to play with a clear mind. The tilt from the day before lingers and makes it more likely that you'll tilt again. Whereas previously it may have taken five or more bad beats to make you just slightly frustrated, just one now sends you to the edge of tilt, and two throws you completely over.

The reason you accumulate this extra anger is because your brain has too much of it to digest. The extra anger weighs on your mind and eventually can force you to stop playing poker in order to clear your mind. For some players, that means taking a few days off, which can be tilting in itself.

If you don't want to take time off, you need to clear out the extra anger that the brain can't process fast enough on its own. You can do that by:

1. *Following the steps to keep poker out of your life on page 91.*

2. *Developing a cool-down routine using the suggestions in Appendix I.*

3. *Using any of the steps to resolve accumulated emotion on page 66.*

Resetting your mind during a bad run isn't just a nice idea, it's a major part of what keeps you playing well while getting hammered.

INJUSTICE TILT

You've been rivered, coolered, and bad beated for the umpteenth time today, and your head is about to explode. You can't believe how unlucky you got. Bad players suck-out in the worst possible spot, regulars run over you, you tilt when you think how much more you could have won, the poker gods have cursed you, you don't deserve this, and you wonder when you're going to get your fair share of good luck. Logic says that variance makes poker profitable. Just be patient, and eventually things will turn in your favor. But the scales of poker justice have tilted against you, and you tilt trying to fight against them.

As the name implies, injustice tilt is about fairness, equity, and justice. While it may seem as if the answer is simply to accept the realities of poker, it's clearly not that simple or this problem would have already been solved. So, as with all other types of tilt, finding the missing logic is key to unlocking a lasting solution.

Answers these questions to help find the missing logic causing your injustice tilt:

- Does it feel like you never get your share of the luck? Or that you're always getting screwed?
- Does it seem as if the money you've lost is being taken from you?
- Is a bad beat, cooler, or suck-out worse when it happens against a fish or a regular?
- What are the situations when bad luck really gets to you?
- Are you jealous or resentful of other players who you think run better than you?
- When variance is really bad, do you wish poker wasn't this way, or that you could somehow control variance?

For many players, at the core of injustice is a feeling that they aren't getting what they think is fair. This begs the question, how do you know what is fair? The mind figures it out by considering the following:

- Variance or luck
- The quality of your skill
- The quality of your opponent's skill

Quite obviously, these three factors together determine your edge in the game, but accurately calculating them isn't easy. The players who do that well have real skill in being able to spot subtle variance, a mistake on their part, or a solid move made by their opponents. While all players have some skill in each area, their skill levels vary dramatically.

Right now, in poker rooms and online, there are players who don't believe the math. They think KK is a better hand preflop than AA, or think they *always* hit their flushes when dealt clubs. Their opinion is of course influenced by the hands they've played so far in their career, and not by statistics. What these players show us (other than they are great opponents to have on your right) is that besides playing badly, bad players also make many errors in how they interpret results. They overestimate their own skill, they have very little understanding about variance or odds, and they think they are better than you or the other regulars at the table.

Errors in interpreting results aren't the exclusive domain of terrible players. Every player has a filter that calculates the influence of variance, their own skill, and their opponent's skill. This filter guides the interpretation of the outcome of a hand, session, tournament, SNGs, etc. It's like a sorting system: variance in this pile, the quality of play in that pile, and opponents' play in the last pile. As the filter sorts results, the totals in each pile automatically give a player a sense of their edge. Injustice tilt develops from fundamental weaknesses or errors in a player's ability to filter results, and that ultimately skews what they believe is fair.

ASSUMING YOU'RE BETTER

Some players falsely assume that losing happens because their opponents were lucky, rather than thinking that they got outplayed. This happens when they have a stronger ability to recognize the quality of their own play than their opponents'. If you can't understand what your opponents are doing, it's logical that you wouldn't give them enough credit and would just believe you're better than them. This subtle bias means that, rather than looking objectively at who's a better player, you automatically assume it's you.

If calculating each of these factors—variance, your skill, opponent skill— was simple, injustice tilt wouldn't exist. Players would easily know what is fair. When you know what is fair, even if you lose, it doesn't feel unjust. Sometimes just the uncertainty of not knowing is enough to drive you mad.

While it's impossible to know definitively in the short term what is fair, there is a skill to it that can improve with work and experience. At first, it may not seem as if you can improve your understanding of variance beyond your aces getting cracked by fives, getting coolered, losing set over set, or constantly running into the top of your opponent's range. Understanding variance is a skill that has already improved from when you first started playing, which means you can continue to understand it even more. *For some advice on how to increase your understanding of variance, go to page 211.*

Justice may be blind and impartial in the courtroom but you are not. In addition to errors in calculating variance, your skill, and your opponent's skill, injustice tilt is exaggerated by the biases that cloud your judgment and tip the scales of justice to automatically rule against you. In other words, you take only small samples of evidence to determine what is fair, and this has a direct impact on how you react at the table.

The major biases in poker are covered in the remainder of this chapter.

Terrible at Spotting Good Variance
Typically, players remember bad luck more than good luck, especially under emotional pressure. Rarely will you hear them tell stories of how they sucked out, but hearing a bad beat story is often unavoidable. Remembering and focusing more on bad luck creates a biased perspective for the simple reason that when you add focus to something, you learn it better. So bad luck gets more attention and thus stands out more easily in your mind. Basically, you're really skilled at spotting bad luck and terrible at spotting good luck.

To make matters worse, not only does this extra focus on bad luck bias your perception overall, when under emotional pressure from a bad run, it's all you remember. So, now a statement such as, "I never get lucky" makes total sense, because bad luck is all you see. In that moment, you truly believe that you never have good luck, and that happens primarily because you're so bad at recognizing it.

More Than Is Fair

When you assume that good luck is actually more of a result of your play and/or assume your mistakes are actually bad luck, and you're wrong these errors bias the scales of poker justice to make variance seem unfair when it's not. The next two figures help to illustrate this point.

Balanced Scale. Figure 1

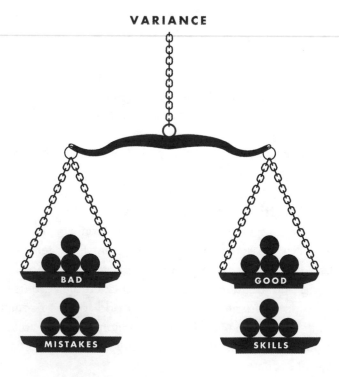

Unbalanced Scale. Figure 2.

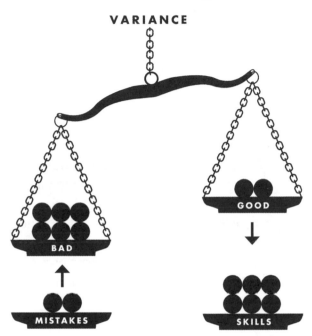

In figure 1, your view of variance is balanced or neutral. You recognize your skill, your mistakes, as well as the skills and mistakes of your opponents. Figure 2 shows how injustice tilt develops. First, if winning actually happens because of good luck, but you believe it was your skill, then some good luck is taken off the scale. Second, if your mistakes cause you to lose, but the loss was presumed to have been caused by bad luck, then some bad luck is added to the scale. By attributing good luck to your skill and your mistakes to bad luck, you believe variance is against you. So in both cases, bad luck appears to happen more frequently, and you tilt believing you're getting screwed, when really you're mentally screwing yourself.

You can imagine when this bias plays out repeatedly over time. It would seem quite reasonable that you'd eventually believe you were cursed, or that variance was unfair if a significant chunk of your winnings were attributed to your skill, but your losses were not. Instead, your losses were attributed to bad luck. In a way, you can consider this to be just a basic math problem, but since each factor is hard to accurately measure, it's far from basic. This is why there's edge to gain by getting better at objectively evaluating your game, your opponent's game, and variance.

Sure, it's hard to identify good luck at times; but as mentioned above, part of the reason is because you don't attribute winning to good luck and you're far more skilled at spotting bad luck. This raises the question, "Why are you trying to make winning in the short run a result of your skill rather than good luck?" It's because you *want* to believe you're as good a player as you think, regardless of whether you actually are that good. This is a confidence problem, and subconsciously the mind knows this pseudo-confidence or overconfidence isn't stable. So, during periods of sustained bad play you'll question your game, lose confidence, and may lose motivation. Refer to chapter 8 for more.

Here are a couple of suggestions for correcting the imbalance in what you believe is fair:

Short term: Improve your ability to spot positive variance and your mistakes. Doing so balances your perspective about variance. *Also refer to page 209 for more about developing the skills of recognizing: variance, your skill, and your opponent's skill.*

Long term: Go back through your poker career, perhaps even your personal, sports, or business life, and identify instances of good luck that at the time you thought happened more because of your skill than variance. Also look for instances when you thought you were getting screwed, but were actually making mistakes. Correcting the bias you have now is easier when you correct your past biases. You can't change what happened in the past, but changing how you look at the past provides a more accurate and stable view of the present.

POKER DOESN'T CARE WHAT YOU THINK IS FAIR.

Injustice Tilt Opportunity

Looking for opportunity in a pile of tilt isn't just about putting a positive spin on things to make you feel better. It's also about finding something of real value that can make you stronger mentally. What are the opportunities?

1. **If you can learn to better handle bad luck today, you'll have an edge over other players—plus it gives you a lead on what can be learned tomorrow.** When you have a lead, it means that you can be working on something else that takes your game even further and keeps you ahead, while others are busy learning how to deal with injustice.

2. **How you handle bad luck can predict how you will handle good luck.** Improving the underlying cause(s) of your injustice tilt also improves how you'll handle a great run. Maintaining balance when it comes to variance is important for more than just bad luck. There are a number of players who rolled through the games during the Chris Moneymaker boom that went bust. They essentially won the poker lottery and couldn't handle it—much the same as people who win the real lottery and go broke soon after.

Wishing Poker Wasn't This Way

When getting to the bottom of why bad luck causes players to tilt, many have admitted that they wish poker didn't have so much variance. Logically, they know variance is a big part of what makes poker so profitable, but that logic isn't enough to satisfy the wish. In fact, there have even been instances when high-profile figures in the game have attempted to create low-or no-variance versions of poker. These attempts have gone down like lead balloons because variance is the very thing that makes poker profitable and fun.

The old adage, "Be careful what you wish for," is true in this case. If you got your wish, and results in the short run were 100% connected to which player was better, what would happen? Since poker is as much a war of the perception of skill as it is of actual skill, action from weaker players would dry up, and poker would become chess.

Assuming that's all true—and many of you already know it is—what's the wish really about? Wishing poker didn't have variance is another way of saying, "I can't handle the emotion variance causes me." If variance didn't cause you to tilt, you'd love that it exists.

Since you can't control variance, the only solution is to:

1. Get better at understanding it. *For more, see page 211.*
2. Improve how you handle it emotionally.

Handling variance better means you accept it. Acceptance happens naturally after learning why you don't want your wish of zero variance to come true.

Desire to Control Variance

The desire to control variance, though it may seem illogical, is deep down something many players want and wish could happen. Often, this comes out in small ways, such as calling for the cards you need, avoiding looking at the flop so as not to jinx the hand, or standing up from your seat during a race. None of this influences the turn of a card, yet you feel it may help in some way. Other times, the desire to control variance is evident in actions such as berating someone who has just sucked out on you, or going as far as getting on your knees and praying like Jerry Yang did (successfully) at the WSOP® Main Event.

Though it may not seem like a big deal, just wishing you could control variance means you're giving up control. Let's assume you have actually run worse than expected and for far longer than the math says is likely.

It's completely reasonable to be pissed off, but the question is whether that frustration or anger affects the quality of your play. Often players with the underlying desire to control variance end up losing control of their game. Since you can't control variance and can only control how you respond to it, the goal is to build up more mental muscle so that you can respond effectively. Of course, it's hard. Variance is a major reason that poker is so challenging. Resolve the desire to control variance, and instead focus on being in more control of your game.

 YOU CAN'T CONTROL VARIANCE, BUT YOU CAN UNDERSTAND IT BETTER.

YOU CAN'T CONTROL THE CARDS. YOU CAN ONLY CONTROL HOW YOU PLAY.

An Excuse Not to Learn

It doesn't take long to find a player who's avoided working on their game because they assumed their losses were due to variance. When it seems like, "there's no point, I'm just going to get screwed again," or if you're an online player obsessed with being down in all-in EV, it's understandable why you wouldn't put in the time. If you believe the reason you're losing is solely due to bad luck, it's actually illogical for you to work on your game—especially when it's much easier to complain.

Frankly, it's easier to complain about bad luck than actually trying to improve because there's less to lose. If you try to improve and still lose, that means you got beat or beat yourself. Both are tough pills to swallow, and can make you feel like you failed, wasted your time, or are a terrible player. Blaming luck essentially helps you avoid these feelings.

The risk of complaining about bad luck is that you tend to ignore your mistakes or the details of how you're being outplayed. This information is essential to improving as a player. By complaining, you shield the reality of your game from yourself. The momentum of this pattern means that the longer it goes on, the more your real edge decreases . . . which increases variance . . . which means more bad luck . . . which means more complaining and less working. This vicious cycle is going to continue until you face the reality of your game and do the work to improve.

There also may be other mental game issues you're protecting yourself from, such as fear of failure, loss of confidence, and mistake tilt. If that's the case, deal directly with those issues as well.

STOP COMPLAINING. THERE IS ALWAYS SOMETHING TO LEARN.

CLIENT'S STORY

Barry Carter
MidStakes SNGs & Cash Games

POKER JOURNALIST

"I had been working as a poker journalist for about five years when I met Jared. Like a lot of people who stick with poker, I ran pretty well in my first few years, but in 2009 I had a pretty brutal downswing that crippled my game. I had heard of Jared and seen his videos, but there was a part of me that thought he was probably going to fill my head with a load of 'visualize yourself not getting bad beats' crap I previously associated with self-help material. But that aside, I was feeling pretty desperate, so I really wanted to try him before I bought a self-help book.

I approached him with essentially three issues. First of all, I felt I was cursed; I really believed I ran worse than anyone else, and was keen to prove it to anyone who would listen. Second, I had developed a terrible case of risk aversion. Finally, I really struggled to work on my game away from the table, and it was an area where I considered myself lazy.

'You know that's a crock of shit, right?' Jared told me.

I was shocked. Wasn't he supposed to be making me feel like I was Phil Ivey and that I could do anything? Can a mental game coach talk to people like that? Weren't we supposed to start Buddhist chants or something?

Jared asked me if I could see how all three issues were clearly linked to each other. I could kind of see the link between feeling cursed and being risk averse, but not at all how being lazy in studying away from the table was linked.

'What's the point of working on your game if you are cursed?' he asked me. 'There is no such thing as lazy; you are simply not motivated to work on your game. You have decided that because you are cursed, you have an excuse not to learn, so you don't.'

All of a sudden it seemed so simple. How did I not notice this before? His opening line calling me out on my crock of shit will always stick with me; it was pretty much then that I realized Jared was the real deal. I have always considered myself to be very self-aware, so for him to have identified why I wasn't working on my game so quickly and clearly had me hooked on the mental game (hence my involvement in this book).

It took a long time to fully crack my reluctance to work on my game, but over the next few months, my own case helped to highlight how most mental game issues are interlinked. My feeling that I was cursed was stopping me from studying, but my risk aversion played a role in it as well. In one particular session, I mentioned to Jared that for me, the 'image' of success in poker is the image of a tournament winner posing for cameras holding their winning two hole cards in front of a mountain of chips.

'I guess I should stop playing cash games and SNGs and start playing tournaments,' I joked.

Never joke during a session with Jared Tendler. He doesn't let it go. He probed me on why, if my image of success is winning a tournament, do I hardly ever play them? Lots of 'Jedi Mind Tricks' later, he made me realize that risk aversion was stopping me from working on my game this time, because I was equating success with something I wasn't even trying to achieve, so I had a perfect excuse when I didn't achieve it.

This ultimately led me to the core of why I wasn't working on my game. I didn't want to put myself in a position where I had to be accountable if I lost. Being a poker journalist, I have to report on successful players every day, and I'm friends with a lot of pros. What I really feared was humiliating myself in front of them, so I took the low-risk route of not working on my game, blaming bad luck, and not leaving myself open to ridicule.

Playing out the fear like this gave me an end point. I knew that the absolute worst thing I could experience if I started to work on my game was ridicule. I also realized from the whole experience that I wasn't nearly as good a player as I thought, which was a good thing, because it meant I could improve. Thanks to some pretty solid learning concepts like the ALM and inchworm, I now know there is always something I can work on, and I have ways of noticing small gradual improvements no matter how bad it gets."

Bad Beat Stories

Bad beat stories are prime examples of injustice tilt, and are a part of the game many players would be happy to see gone. Players hate being told these stories, yet after a sick beat are compelled to tell one, too.

Why do players who knowingly hate to tell bad beat stories continue to do so?

- They're looking for confirmation that it was as terrible as they think.
- It's a form of competition to see who has the worst story.
- They're looking for something to blame.
- It's a reason not to work on their game.
- They're looking for pity, sympathy, or commiseration.
- Sometimes they do make pretty great stories (in a sick way).

For some players, resolving the need to tell these stories is a result of addressing other parts of this chapter. If this isn't the case, figure out why you tell bad beat stories using the list above, and fix it.

Jealousy

Injustice tilt is a form of tilt that can develop and accumulate without even playing a hand. The feeling that you're not getting your fair share of good fortune can also come from seeing other players get more than what you think is fair. Some successful players are thought to simply run extremely hot, and little or no consideration is given to their ability or how hard they work on their game.

For instance, some believe the success of such big names as Gus Hansen is due to luck and not at all to skill. So when you think of the millions of dollars he's won and titles he holds, it seems incomprehensible and unfair how much he wins compared to you. Jealousy also can happen when a close poker friend, who you think you're just as good as, is making a real name for himself. Seeing what he's winning makes it seem as if you should be having the same level of success.

To start making improvements on the issue of jealousy, answer the following questions:

1. What do others have that you wish you had?
2. What would having it mean for you?

3. What more can you be doing that you aren't already? (There's always something, even if it's just having patience.)

4. What have you achieved that hasn't been celebrated enough?

Your answers provide insight into what needs more focus, allowing you to be less focused on the fortune of others. Also, since players with stable confidence have fewer problems with jealousy, read chapter 8.

HATE-LOSING TILT

Losing is a reality in any competitive environment. This is especially true in poker where variance is built into the fabric of the game. Nowhere other than poker does the better player—even the best in the world—lose so often because of variance.

How you lose a hand matters, but it matters less than the simple reality that you lost. Lose one hand and your frustration spikes like a mild tremor on the Richter scale. Then as losses pile up, frustration steadily builds into tilt—unless you lose in a particularly vicious way and then a full-blown tiltquake happens instantly.

Most everyone reading this section knows that variance is part of the game. You'd like to be friends with it, but deep down you hate it. Logically you know that variance is part of what makes poker so profitable, but since that logic isn't enough to stop this kind of tilt, there must be more pieces to this puzzle.

When logic isn't enough, there usually are some other nuggets of information that aren't being accounted for and require a little digging to discover. The important first question to ask: Why do you hate losing?

- **Is it the feeling?** Losing often feels terrible, can go on for a while, and even affects other aspects of your life.

- **Is it the money?** Winning money is ultimately how you're measured in poker, so it makes sense why you'd hate losing it.

No one's ever going to pump their fist to celebrate losing a big pot or busting out of a tournament, but the following sections can at least help you make peace with losing.

Competitiveness

No matter what you're competing for, being competitive is a great trait. It's one shared by many successful poker players, athletes, and business-people. Competition naturally brings out a strong desire to win, and that's a great thing. Being competitive in poker is not inherently a problem. Wanting to win money, beat your opponents, and profit every session are solid goals. They just aren't entirely in your control in the short run.

Everyone agrees that there are situations when you lose to bad players that are actually extremely profitable spots in the long run. Logically you understand this, but in the moment when you lose, it's hard to see the bigger picture.

To find out why losing is such a problem, it's often easier to first look at what you gain from winning besides money. Every time you play poker, there is more on the line than just money—it's worth taking some time to define what's on the line for you. Here are some examples:

- Being better than your opponent(s).
- Ability to pay the bills.
- Achievement and accomplishment of poker goals.
- Respect from people who think you're wrong for even playing poker.
- Confidence in your game.
- Ability to move up in stakes.

- Others' opinions of your game.
- The time, energy, and work you put into the game.
- The better chance of retiring early.

There is more than just money on the line when you play; you're competing for what's on this list, and more. It's as if each one is bet along with the actual money on the table. When you lose, it's not just money that's gone—you've also lost confidence, respect from others, progress towards your goals, or anything else on your list. You hate losing because you're competing for so much more than you realize.

Losing also feels worse when you assume more losses will happen in the future, and it feels even worse when you can't imagine ever winning again. This prediction of the future fans the downward spiral of tilt. When you believe more losses are to come in the future, you have more to be pissed off about in the present.

Solving this type of tilt begins with a better definition of the real problem. Being competitive is not the problem. Being frustrated at losing is not the problem. You have goals, there's a lot on the line, and being frustrated when it doesn't go your way means you care about what you're investing into the game. Plus, frustration at low levels can be fuel to perform and can motivate you to work harder away from the table. Successful athletes in major sports channel their frustration in this way all the time, but that can only happen when the excess layers that turn it into anger, hate, or rage, are removed.

Together with reviewing the other sections in this chapter, consider the following to help you define the cause and the solution of your hatred of losing:

1. **Define winning.** Since winning is about more than just money, take a closer look at the other things that are in play, and define what winning means for each one. This is especially important for

things that are harder to calculate than money, such as respect, effort, and achievement. For example: How are you going to know when you can actually move up in stakes? Winning means you have a 60 buy-in bankroll. When will others respect you for playing poker? Winning means you've supported yourself for five years and if they don't respect you then, it's their problem. How do you know if you're better than your opponents? Winning means having a better win-rate or head-to-head record over a large sample.

Write out the definitions of what winning means for everything that's on the line for you when you play. Then reread these to remind yourself of them before you play. The tendency is to automatically assume that when you lose, you're also losing along all of these lines too; but that may not be true. You may actually be winning and not even realize it.

2. **Drop the assumption that losing will continue**. The assumption that you will lose is a mental flaw that means you believe your predictions for the future will always be 100% accurate. They won't be. To counteract this, do the following at a time when you're relaxed or at least not pissed off:

Look at the high and low points of your results at different points in your career, such as six months ago, two years ago, and even farther back. Doing this helps you gain perspective. When losing in the past, you assumed losing would continue, but it didn't. Remind yourself of this fact regularly and you'll take away a layer of frustration that otherwise would accumulate.

 DON'T LET VARIANCE BEAT YOU BY FORCING YOU TO PLAY BADLY.

Money Lost

Another reason you hate losing is your belief that the money lost is gone forever. (This is especially true for Heads Up players after getting hit and run.) Rather than just thinking of money as something that's won or lost each time you play, consider it to be an investment in your edge that yields a return over time. Thinking in this way may sound logical, but the fact that you are tilting when losing money proves you're more concerned about short-term losses than the bigger picture.

Rather than thinking in terms of money won or lost, take a lesson from the business world. In many businesses, there is a major difference between the money being held and the money that's actually earned as income. For example, a retail store offering a refund within 30 days realizes the income of a sale after the 30-day period is over, not on the day of the sale. Until that point, the money is just being held and is not considered income. In poker, if you believe *all* the money won in the short run is yours—especially on a great run of cards—then predictably you'll get pissed off when poker takes back what you really didn't earn. Often the seeds of hating to lose are planted when you assume more of what you won to be income.

Unlike a retail business, poker makes it difficult to know if money lost is truly gone forever or whether it's just an investment in your edge. To counteract this, some players try thinking about their earn rate: If they've lost a buy-in over an hour they instead have made their average hourly rate of $X. If thinking in these terms helps, then keep doing it. Just be sure to leave some wiggle room in your mind, so that by the time you figure out what you actually earned over that period, you aren't disappointed if your income is lower than expected.

Some players believe using an hourly rate is a way to rationalize losing. In small samples it is, but the larger the size of the sample your earn rate is based on, the more reliable it becomes. Whether you use it or not, at a minimum, don't assume money won in the short run is yours until you can prove you've earned it.

INJECTING LOGIC

THE MONEY ON THE TABLE IS AN INVESTMENT IN YOUR EDGE. IF YOU LOST MAKING PROFITABLE PLAYS, LOSING IS TEMPORARY AS LONG AS YOU KEEP PLAYING WELL AND IMPROVING.

CLIENT'S STORY

Jordan "iMsoLucky0" Morgan
Tournament player & Mid-stakes NLHE
FULL TILT POKER RED PRO

"When I met Jared, I already had a lot of tournament success and a sponsorship deal with Full Tilt. I wanted to get into cash games, but was having trouble not tilting. I was chasing losses, jumping limits, and basically being a degenerate gambler. If I lost, I would tell myself, 'I have to get that money back; I have to get even; I can do this; I have control'–but it was the long run, not short run that I controlled, and when I realized that, a lot of my problems were solved.

Improvement came quite instantly. Just understanding what was going on in my head solved a lot of the problem. Incorporating a warm-up before I played, and journaling at the end also helped me to identify my own tilt patterns, which made it easier to deal with them sooner and more effectively. Now, I am calmer, more of a realist, less of an idealist, and understand that these things have to happen in poker."

INJECTING LOGIC
"I CAN'T ALWAYS PLAY PERFECTLY. I CAN ONLY PLAY MY BEST."

"EVEN THOUGH IT DOESN'T SEEM LIKE IT RIGHT NOW, I AM BEATING THE GAMES . . . BUT I DON'T HAVE MUCH OF AN EDGE WHEN TILTING."

Believing You Can Win Every Hand

Though logically it's hard for a player to admit to believing that they can win every hand or every session, there are many who actually do. It sounds illogical because of course they know better; variance would never allow such a thing to happen. Knowing that this belief is illogical still isn't enough to stop players from clinging to the idea that one day they'll become so good they'll never lose.

Poker does a great job of feeding this belief. When you run hot, the game seems like an ATM dispensing out money. It starts to really seem as if you win every hand. It feels great to win and to play that well, especially when the run goes on longer. Winning that much brings out dreams of what it would be like to be so good that you never lose. In a similar way to the dreams people have about winning the lottery, images emerge in your mind of what you would do with the money or what it would mean for your life.

Of course, this is poker, not the lottery. While a few recent WSOP® Main Event winners seem to have won poker's version of the lottery, if it were possible for you or anyone else to be *that* good, poker would cease to be as profitable. The fact that you can't win every single time is precisely why you can find games where you have an edge, with inferior players willing to play you. Poker isn't an ATM; it's more like a slot machine calibrated to pay out your edge (minus the rake). Earning your edge means you have to pay out a lot of what you take in—sometimes in dramatic fashion.

If running well makes you think it's easy to win money in poker, then you'll hate when you inevitably lose because losing destroys your dream. The solution to this problem has to include improving how you handle winning, as much as improving how you handle losing. That begins with ditching the dream of easy money. Also, try the following to eliminate the belief that you can win every hand or every session:

- **Preparation:** Reinforce your focus on making good decisions, reading the actions, and anything else needed to play well. Remember why losing is an important part of poker, and why money saved from good lay downs is as good as money won. While this may become repetitive, mastery of the solution eventually means the flaw is resolved and no longer requires your attention. Until that point, keep working at it.

- **Performance:** If losing one hand causes even minor frustration, inject logic after each loss. Doing so prevents emotion from accumulating as much, and delays tilt. Since winning is also part of the problem, when emotions start to get *too positive*, inject logic then, too.

IT'S NOT POSSIBLE TO WIN EVERY HAND; YOUR FOCUS NEEDS TO BE ON PLAYING EVERY HAND WELL.

- **Evaluation:** Whether this problem shows up from winning or losing, use the mental hand history to reinforce the breakdown of faulty logic and the buildup of the correction.

- **Break your wish of easy money:** Prove to yourself why you don't want this wish to come true. Then each time you have dreams about it, redirect your thoughts or actions to something productive that you can actually achieve.

Lost Skill

Players often fall into a trap where they believe that losing money also means their skill has disappeared. When losing and on tilt, they suddenly think they suck. This is just an illusion of the mind. Skills learned to the level of Unconscious Competence are owned and never disappear—even when on tilt.

This illusion arises for three reasons:

1. Equating money with skill. If you lose money, and money equals skill, then you instantly suck when you lose. You'll also hate losing because when other players are winning you believe they can suddenly be that much better. If it's possible for your skill to suddenly disappear, their skill can instantly appear.

2. Unconscious Competence skills are unconscious—by definition you don't have to think about them, and consequently they are taken for granted.

3. Skills in the process of being learned don't show up when on tilt, and can seem to have disappeared—possibly forever—along with the rest of your game.

Here's how to break this illusion:

1. **Improve the skill of recognizing: variance, your skill, and your opponent's skill.** Then when you lose, you can determine how you actually played, rather than just assuming you suck. Plus, if you played well, it will feel good to know you were able to even on a tough day. *See page 211 for more.*

2. **Know the solid parts of your game that are trained to the level of Unconscious Competence.** While these are basic skills, just knowing them proves your entire game can't disappear, even while on tilt.

Losing Gets Personal

Competing against other players—especially Heads Up—makes winning a personal challenge in which there's a lot more at stake than just money. Losing means they got the better of you, and they're the ones who get to feel superior, not you; even if they just got lucky. It can be tilting just thinking that another player, especially a weaker one, believes they are better than you. If it also happens against someone you have a history with, then tilt is even worse.

While your actions may not turn into revenge tilt, the discussion and strategies starting on page 135 are relevant enough to help you solve this version of hate-losing tilt.

Losing Hurts More Than Winning Feels Good

For many players, losing feels worse than winning feels good (Prospect Theory[2]). That means they're not only competing to win, they're also competing to avoid the negative feelings that come with losing. Competitive people can be really hard on themselves when they lose. Self-criticism can show up in many ways, such as rhetorically asking, "Why do I suck so bad?" or "How am I ever going to be any good if I can't beat this jackass?" Regardless of how self-criticism shows up, it combines with the other factors described in this section to make losing hurt badly—in fact badly enough that winning never feels equally as good and becomes more of an escape from the torture of losing.

Players who see winning as an escape from losing are the same ones who think the answer to the pain of losing is to just win ("If I just win everything will be fine"). Winning temporarily allows you to avoid the agony of defeat, but since losing is guaranteed to happen as long as you play poker, it's better to solve the real problem than to stick a bandage on it.

The real problem here is there are more reasons to feel bad about losing than reasons to feel good about winning. Consequently, you anticipate losing to feel more negative—and when that's true, it tilts you even more. By reducing the unnecessary and flawed reasons that losing hurts, the pattern observed by Prospect Theory goes away.

---

2   Kahneman, Daniel, and Amos Tversky (1979) "Prospect Theory: An Analysis of Decision under Risk", *Econometrica*, XLVII (1979), 263-291

The first step in breaking this pattern is to know that Prospect Theory is an observation, not a law of human nature. This pattern is real, it just isn't permanent. To improve it, resolve the reasons why losing hurts more than winning by using the methods described previously in this section.

MISTAKE TILT

Learning means making mistakes. When you aren't making mistakes, it's because you already know what's correct.

At a basic level, being frustrated for making a mistake is reasonable. You have goals in poker, and it sucks to perform poorly. Being frustrated by mistakes isn't necessarily a problem, and can even be a good thing when it provides motivation to actually do the work to fix it. What distinguishes mistake tilt as a problem is frustration that is so intense that it affects your play, leads to more mistakes, and ultimately makes it harder to fix the mistakes you're making.

Mistake tilt is something you may not even realize you experience, as it's often hidden by more obvious reasons to tilt; for instance, bad beats and running bad. Also, players don't routinely talk about hating mistakes, even though many do. Only when they are asked direct questions about making mistakes does it becomes clear that their mistakes caused them to tilt.

Since the issue is obscure, to help identify whether it's a problem for you, here are some statements made by players who hate mistakes when asked, "What is it about making mistakes that makes you so angry?"

- "It feels like such a waste of time and money."
- "It's going to take a long time to make up for it."
- "It makes me feel like a failure."
- "It means I'm not as good as I thought."
- "It's inexcusable to be making such obvious mistakes at this point in my career."

- "I've put the time in; I should have known better."
- "I'm never going to be a great player if I keep making the same stupid mistakes over and over!"
- "It feels like I've taken a huge step backwards."
- "It's worse when already on tilt because the mistakes are so basic."
- "I'm concerned what others (players, coach, friends) will think."
- "I just erased a day's work with one stupid f*&%ing move!"

Embedded within each of these statements are the underlying reasons why mistakes cause players to tilt. The remainder of this chapter breaks down the common underlying reasons for mistake tilt, making it easier for you to resolve. While there are several underlying reasons, they are all connected in some way to fundamental errors in your understanding of the learning process and the nature of performance. Mistakes are essential to improving as a player; in essence, by hating them you hate improving. Of course very few people think in that way, but your reaction shows that at the level of Unconscious Competence you hate mistakes. When these errors are corrected, it not only means that mistake tilt goes away, but you're also going to be better at fixing poker mistakes and learning the game in general. Ultimately you'll become a stronger player.

When mistakes are viewed as a problem, they naturally cause tilt—especially when they continue to happen in big spots, when moving up in stakes, or against a regular who you can never beat. As you analyze your reasons why mistakes cause you to tilt, also keep in mind the situations that make your tilt worse, and why.

Expecting Perfection

You manage to unlock everything you have been working on and play an incredible session or tournament, or get on a longer streak of perfect play. You've reached a new height in your game where great play has become the standard and now you expect this new standard to show up every time you play. Mistakes and poor play have become a distant memory, and no longer even seem possible. Unfortunately, reaching new heights in your game doesn't come with much satisfaction since it was expected, and now any mistake (no matter how slight) is met with wrath. You either feel neutral about playing perfectly, or you beat yourself senseless at the slightest presence of a mistake. That seems fair?!

Perfect play is a moving target that is attainable at times. However, it's not possible to achieve a permanent poker nirvana where poker is easy forever. The simple reason that can't happen is that your best gets better and your definition of perfection increases. Essentially, when you achieve a new peak in your game, your newly minted A-game pushes your old A-game to your B-game, and your old B-game becomes your C-game. Having your skill set continually moving along as though on a conveyer belt is the nature of how improvement happens over time. On a larger scale, the game evolves when thousands of poker players go through this process.

The roots of mistake tilt begin to take hold when at your peak. You've found permanent perfection . . . a poker paradise where you never make mistakes and the game is easy. Only you're forgetting it's an illusion; the last time you reached a peak, you thought you found nirvana only to realize you still have weaknesses. It can be easy to believe that weaknesses don't exist while at the top of your game and that's why making a mistake is so frustrating: You weren't expecting to make one, even though it was bound to happen.

The way to reach your next peak is by correcting weaknesses. As the concept of inchworm illustrates, the underlying weaknesses in your game that cause mistakes have to be corrected for the back end of your range to take a step forward. Only when your worst has improved are you able to take steps toward the next peak in your game. Rather than expect perfection, keep striving for it by continually correcting your mistakes.

Lastly, when you expect perfection, there's an assumption that you already know the correction and how to subtly apply it to all the unique situations in which that mistake happens. Basically, you are assuming that you have already mastered the correction, but making a mistake proves that you haven't. This is the real mistake in the situation.

To correct problems with perfectionism, try the following:

1. **Gain a more realistic view of the learning process so you can prove why perfection cannot be attained all the time.** With stronger knowledge about learning, you automatically won't expect perfection, and instead can have it as a goal. Review chapter 2 for more.

2. **When you play perfectly, feel good about it.** Reaching the top of your game deserves some recognition since you've worked hard to get there. Playing perfectly is not expected; it's a goal. Recognizing what you've accomplished doesn't mean you have to get caught up reveling in your own greatness; you just need to feel good about it.

3. **When you play perfectly, also take a close look at how you got there.** Knowing how you achieve results strengthens your ability to achieve future results. Plus, if you eliminate weaknesses in your approach to learning and performance, such as distractions, procrastination, or mistake tilt, then you become more efficient when striving for the next peak and can get there faster.

 INJECTING LOGIC

MISTAKES ARE GOING TO HAPPEN. THE BIGGER MISTAKE IS LETTING ONE TURN INTO MORE.

When a Mistake Is Not a Mistake

Poker is inherently a game of deception. Unfortunately, the deception extends to your perception of your game. Run hot and you think you played great; run bad, or just even lose one hand, and you think you played terribly. While this kind of deception is a major reason why poker is so profitable, it also causes a unique type of mistake tilt.

Players often think they've made a mistake while playing only to realize afterward that their decision was actually close and perhaps not a mistake at all. Thinking you make mistakes wouldn't be a problem if it didn't then lead to tilt (and ultimately, making real mistakes). So oddly enough, to cause this type of mistake tilt, you just have to think you make a mistake, and not actually make one.

Therefore, being able to know when a mistake is actually a mistake is the key to eliminating this type of tilt. If you want to stop yourself from going on tilt and spewing money in this way, the solution is to fix the *real* mistake—your inability to recognize mistakes in real time.

It sounds simple enough, but can you name the weaknesses or common mistakes in your game right now? If not, then you don't know the weak parts of your game well enough to spot them as they happen. Here's how to correct your inability to recognize mistakes while playing:

1. **Analyze the full range of your game, from your best to your absolute worst.** Write out the mistakes made when tilted, tired, autopiloting, and distracted. Next, write down the mistakes made when you're playing poorly, but not that bad. Finally, write down your standard B-game mistakes. Work on the list for a few weeks, adding to it after each time you play, before finalizing it.

   Study it, and then at the table when you see a certain mistake show up, you'll get instant feedback on how well you're actually playing. If you don't make any of these mistakes, then you can continue to focus on playing well. If you lose the hand, it's either due to variance, or a new mistake that you couldn't have known about and can't analyze while playing. Take note of the hand, move on, and stay focused on playing well.

2. **Regularly evaluate your game to keep your understanding up-to-date.** Over time, as the worst aspects of your game are eliminated, take them off of your list. Then when new mistakes show up in your B-game, add them to your list. This way, you have a steady stream of things to work on.

 JUST BECAUSE YOU LOST THE HAND, DOESN'T MEAN YOU PLAYED IT BADLY.

Obvious Mistakes

An obvious mistake is, well, obvious—and that's the problem. It's not a close decision that could have gone either way; it's blatantly obvious and so incredibly stupid and incomprehensible that you can barely believe it just happened. Since an obvious mistake usually happens because you're already tilting—autopilot and overconfidence being two other big reasons—making such a boneheaded mistake causes the tilt of tilt and throws you completely over the edge. For some, this may be the first sign that they're actually on tilt.

This kind of a mistake is hard to wrap your head around because it seems so wildly out of character for your game. If you keep playing, mistakes continue to pile up, and tilt continues to rise until you eventually quit—but the problem doesn't end there. Then begins the aftermath of trying to make sense of how the hell this could have happened. As you struggle to come up with an answer beyond, "I'm an idiot tilt monkey," the next few days are a struggle because it's tough to get the mistake out of your head while trying to relax, hanging with friends, sleeping, and playing in future sessions. Correcting an obvious mistake is a challenge for sure, but as with any other problem, the correction starts by knowing what caused it.

The mistakes are obvious to you because of how severe the gap is between these mistakes and your normal game. The decisions you make when emotions rise too high because of tilt, or are too low when autopiloting, bored, or tired, are made using the knowledge of poker that you've mastered to the level of Unconscious Competence. Regardless of what you may think you've mastered, the skills that disappear do so because you hadn't learned them to that level yet.

There's more. Since the mistakes you're making are so basic, it is very likely that accumulated tilt or another mental game leak is preventing them from being corrected to the level of Unconscious Competence. It's as if accumulated tilt is a worker on an assembly line holding up production. Instead of a final product, you're left with an unfinished pile. In this case, poker knowledge is stuck in the process of being learned, and is being held short of getting to Unconscious Competence. As a result, you are forced to think about all of the new poker knowledge in order to be good at it—Conscious Competence. When thinking stops, as it does when tilting or autopiloting, you have no chance of being able to play correctly in these spots, and an obvious mistake happens.

Here's how to stop making obvious mistakes:

1. **Revisit the ALM and inchworm, and the section "Malfunctioning Mind."** These sections explain how an obvious mistake can happen. Once you know why it happens, the extra layer of anger created by not knowing then disappears. This means you can focus on fixing either your accumulated tilt or any other mental game problem, and can correct the obvious mistake.

2. **After making an obvious mistake, decide whether to keep playing or to quit.** If you decide to keep playing, work hard to reduce the mental game mistake (tilt, autopilot, overconfidence, etc.) that caused it, so you can focus on playing as well as you can.

3. **Prioritize improving the mental game leak that leads to making such obvious mistakes.** Otherwise, you have very little chance of correcting these mistakes.

Threatens Your Goals

You want to be playing up at Rail Heaven or winning bracelets, but making mistakes, especially obvious ones, seems like a big setback in achieving that dream. When the following reactions happen after tilting because of mistakes, it's because your poker goals are under attack:

- "I can't believe I just wasted my time and money."
- "I just erased everything I'm working for."
- "I've failed."
- "I'm never going to be a great player if I keep making these mistakes."

When you have a flawed understanding of the learning process, it means you also have a flawed understanding of how to achieve goals. Expectations rise too high, and you end up thinking you can do more in less time. When mistakes happen, naturally, tilt shows up because it seems as if your goals are being destroyed. It seems as if you're failing, and your goals can't be achieved, but really the mistake is a lack of understanding about the learning process.

Correct this problem by understanding more about learning and by removing any flaws in how you set goals. *For more about setting goals, read page 192.*

Know Too Much, Mastered Too Little

With the massive amount of poker education now available, it's easy for players to want to gain more knowledge than their skill can handle. With so much available to learn, players can end up being too liberal in what they define as a mistake. It's like a teenager driving a racecar soon after learning to drive—all that technology would be too much for their basic skill level. If that driver were to crash, is it a mistake? No. Mistakes are only mistakes relative to their range (bell curve and inchworm). Here's a purposefully dramatic example to prove this point:

> A $25/$50 regular evaluating the game of a $0.50/$1 player to their standard identifies mistakes the weaker player can't even comprehend. The stronger player sees flaws in how they balance their range, size up their bets, play the turn, level the regulars, and much more. So if the $.50/$1 player tries to correct the mistakes spotted by the $25/$50 regular, it's the equivalent of trying to run before they can even walk. The $0.50/$1 player is going to be much better off applying knowledge relevant to the level they are playing.

New knowledge is built upon a foundation of the old. You don't suddenly learn about G-Bucks calculations when you start at $100NL. You first learn about ascribing ranges and equity calculations to get a strong understanding of mathematics in poker. Learning poker is much like progressing through the belts in karate. In order to perform higher-level concepts, you must first master concepts in the level below. Unlike karate, your poker education may not be so organized that you can be certain of what to learn next.

Whether the problem is disorganization, or consuming too much information, this type of mistake tilt develops because you know about more poker concepts theoretically than you can actually apply while playing. Basically, you have too much to think about and too little mastered to the level of Unconscious Competence. When you achieve mastery of the basic parts of your game, you free up mental space to apply advanced concepts.

As with many other causes of mistake tilt, the solution is to build a strong knowledge base for the learning process and organize your learning. Working steadily through poker's equivalent of karate belts gives you the best chance not only to avoid tilt, but to sustain a high learning curve.

ENTITLEMENT TILT

At the root of entitlement tilt is the belief that you have the right or deserve to win for such reasons as working harder, being smarter, and having a longer career than your opponents. It's classic Phil Hellmuth tilt. He often reacts in ways that suggest he believes his previous accomplishments have earned him the right to win, regardless of how he currently plays.

Entitlement tilt happens when something you believe to be rightfully yours has been taken. Winning is a possession that you *already* own and when inevitable losses mount, it's as if you've been robbed by someone not deserving of winning—either a regular or a fish.[3] Often the first signs after losing are disbelief, shock, or even laughter because you can't believe what just happened. Soon after, or as losses pile up, tilt sets in and players have thoughts or make statements such as:

- "The cards shouldn't matter. I can outplay them."
- "This guy sucks. How can I possibly lose to him!?"
- "I'm too good to allow that to happen."
- "This guy doesn't even belong at the same table as me."
- "Other players don't work as hard as I do."
- "I'm supposed to win against fish."
- "I have a great track record and do all the right things."
- "I work harder, I'm better. How the f@&% can I be losing here!?"

The real problem with entitlement tilt isn't that you believe you are a better player than your opponents. In many cases, that's probably true. The real problem is that you believe being a better player means you should *never* lose. Pay close attention to what this belief is essentially saying about your mindset and the real issue emerges: overconfidence.

---

3   You never feel entitled against players you know are better than you.

Overconfidence

Overconfidence means that your confidence is exaggerated or inflated because you believe things about your game or ability that aren't true. The belief that being better than your opponents means you should never lose is unrealistic. Therefore, if your confidence is based on this belief, it is not based on reality. While having confidence is important, it must be based on real ability. Believing you should never lose to your opponents creates false confidence.

Poker does a good job of feeding false beliefs to your confidence. A great run not only pads your bankroll, it pads your confidence—unfortunately, in artificial ways for both. Players with entitlement tilt very often assume things that aren't real during a great run. They may think:

1. More of the great run is a direct result of their game than it actually is.

2. They actually own another player's souls. Really it's their deeper understanding of their game (plus good cards) that produces their control of the situation; but subtly it feels as if they control them. *For more, on this illusion of control go to pages 144 and 218.*

3. They have achieved poker nirvana and become the great player they imagined was possible.

When a good run fuels your dreams of how good of a poker player you can be, you're set up to tilt when poker slaps you awake. You're a mental fish when you believe you should never lose.

Another common exaggerated belief that shows up during a great run is, "I feel like I can beat anyone." While it may *feel* as if you can beat anyone, you can't[4]; and believing you can without a sick run of cards is a dream. The positive emotions around this belief are so strong, it *feels* as if you can take on all comers. You can't. You aren't really that good of a

---

4   Unless you're among the best players in the world at a particular game.

player. Variance has inflated your confidence and now you're primed for tilt when you lose. Wanting to win isn't a problem. The problem is that you believe the lie that says you have a right to win all the time.

Believing you deserve to win or that you can beat anyone often hides real weaknesses in how you're playing. Since in your mind, winning is already yours, it would be illogical to put in the work necessary to correct the weaknesses in your game. Recognizing these weaknesses would be a blow to your confidence. It would mean you aren't as good as you thought. So in order to remain confident, you tell yourself these lies:

- "They got lucky."
- "They don't deserve to win."
- "I win because I play well."
- "If I suck-out, it's because I made the right play."
- "I know I work harder than them; I deserve to win."
- "This guy sucks."
- "I played solid."

These are attempts to protect your false confidence. You want to believe you're *that* good. However, if it were true that you deserved to win because you're smarter, better, or work harder, it would mean you also believe the rules of variance don't apply to you. You know variance is part of the game, but deep down you believe (or wish) you are above it.

Once exposed, players often feel relieved that they no longer have to protect these lies. Freed to focus on their game in a real way, they use the mental energy that was previously protecting their confidence to identify and improve their poker weaknesses. It can be tough to face the weaknesses in your game, but it's better than pretending they don't exist.

To reduce overconfidence, do the following:

1. **Use the mental hand history to eliminate the lies in your game.** When you find the correct answers, study them regularly so you can work toward mastering the truth. The better you know the correction, the less you believe the lies, and the more you can control your anger.

2. **Inject logic when confidence is rising too high.** To reduce overconfidence, use the same strategy that you use to reduce tilt. The only difference is that you're keeping an eye out for the signs that your confidence is rising too high and injecting logic when you notice these signs.

3. *Go to page 208 for more information and advice about overconfidence.*

 YOU PLAYED WELL, VARIANCE JUST GAVE YOU MORE MONEY. IT DOESN'T MEAN YOU DESERVE ALL OF IT.

Losing to Fish

It seems illogical to be pissed off about losing to fish. You know they have to win in the short term, yet for some reason it still tilts you. As a player with a huge edge against fish, it makes sense why you would expect to win and consequently tilt when you lose. The problem is you're equating the level of variance in poker with the level of variance in sports.

In major pro sports, such as golf, soccer, baseball, and basketball, when there are large differences in skill between players or teams, variance has little to no effect on the outcome. A professional sports team never loses to an opponent with the level of skill that's analogous to the fish in poker (unless they're competing in a charity event). There isn't enough variance in those sports for it to happen. In baseball, numerous bad calls by umpires will not help a high school team beat the New York Yankees. In golf, the weather and course terrain contribute a lot of variance, but Tiger Woods would never lose to an average country club golfer—not even if Tiger had to use three clubs and hit every shot from his knees. Examples like this are true in every major sport, including mental sports, but they stop with poker. Nowhere else do vastly superior players lose at a higher rate in the short term.

As a player with superior skill, you may not realize that entitlement tilt happens when you make the same mistake that a weaker player would make. Poker is partially a battle of the perception of skill. A big part of your profit comes from your opponents miscalculating their actual skill and sitting in games where they are insurmountable underdogs. Winning against you and other regulars helps fuel misconceptions in how they view their skill. They think they're good enough to have a chance against you, while you think your edge is so big that you should win all the time. You and the fish both make errors in calculating your respective skill level. Your errors cause tilt when you lose.

CLIENT'S STORY

Liz "RikJamesB1atch" Herrera
Heads Up NL up to $50/$100

"I would become incredibly frustrated when I would lose to weaker opponents. It would wreck my whole day. Then Jared opened my eyes by having me think about this idea of me being like a casino. He said, 'You have to expect to lose in order to keep your customers coming back.' Every time I started getting tilty, I would think of this and it got me back to playing well. Now it seems obvious, but when I'm so consumed with frustration I never think of stuff like that."

Losing to Regulars

When losing against other regulars, you might think, say, or feel something like this:

- "I hate when they think they're better than me."
- "They do things so blatantly bad. I have no respect for their game."
- "I know I've worked harder than this guy."
- "I know I'm better."
- "They must have gotten lucky."
- "I hate when the terrible plays they make cost me money."

The central reason why you tilt losing to regulars is the same as why you tilt losing to fish: miscalculating your skill. It's just in a slightly more complex way.

Among regulars, the edges are small and more difficult to clearly define. Players often rely on a feeling or a sense that they have about their edge against other regulars. This sense is something that's indefinable in practical, real, or objective terms, but they're convinced it's true. Not having actual proof of your edge doesn't mean that your gut feeling is wrong. However, if you are relying on a feeling to define your edge, you must take into account the underlying flaws that cause entitlement tilt.

If you believe you have an edge but can't prove it, you're relying on a feeling or sense to define it. Remember, though, that your opinion is biased by the underlying cause of why you tilt when losing to a regular. You *want* to believe you're the better player, and this flaw makes your opinion unreliable. It very well may be true that you are a better player, but without proof to back up this feeling, you're gambling.

Knowing how you stack up against your opponents is a huge part of poker, and it's actually a skill you need to improve along with your technical skills. The stronger this skill, the more clearly you can define your edge, and the less influence negative results have on your mindset.

Without this skill, you lack the hard evidence to back up the belief you have about your edge.

Here are a couple of strategies to help resolve entitlement tilt:

1. **Rather than *feeling* as if you're a better player, prove it.** Do this by improving your ability to determine who has more skill between you and the other regulars. It may seem impossible, but as with any other skill, it becomes stronger the more you work on it. Plus, just by working on it, you're already thinking in a way that prevents entitlement tilt from showing up. *For more, go to page 212.*

2. **Avoid getting caught believing your opponents don't improve.** Often there are two hidden beliefs within entitlement tilt that cause even more anger:

   1. You will always be better.
   2. They will always suck.

   Poker players make shitty psychics. Most likely, other regulars are going to improve. If you're a better player right now that doesn't mean you always will be. Assume they'll improve, and put in the necessary work to stay ahead of them.

CLIENT'S STORY

Mike "Syous" Song
High Stakes HU NL/PLO Specialist
DEUCESCRACKED COACH

"I started getting coached by Jared after a really tough stretch where I broke even for four months. I thought being a successful Heads Up player it would be easy to make money; but after losing for so long I just felt defeated. As the sessions got worse and worse, I would play less and less. I started to tilt much easier, and even had a black mark on my hand from punching the desk in frustration. It was really stressful.

I started using Jared's advice and I immediately made some improvement . . . that was, until I tilted off $22,000 in one session. Normally I would have gotten really down about it, but I tried to hold off judgment until I could talk with Jared and figure out what the hell happened. The problem was, I thought I deserved to win versus this one player. I was super arrogant, but didn't even realize it until we analyzed my mindset. Jared quickly reminded me that I didn't deserve anything in poker. I couldn't just show up and expect to win. If I did, I deserved what was coming.

He also said something that was really funny: 'You're acting like Phil Hellmuth.' That was such an insult to me, it even sent a chill down my spine; he is the last guy I want to be like. Now it's a great reminder to tell myself, 'You're being Phil Hellmuth.' I really understand now that the only thing I can do is play my best, and Jared helped me see how arrogance could destroy my game.

So, I decided to treat that one opponent in the complete opposite way as I did the first time—as if he was the better player and studied his game earnestly. I dissected the hand histories for three hours, and the next time we played I had a $24,000 day. I'm now up $30,000 in total against him and haven't seen him at the tables in a while.

In general, I now spend a lot more time working on my game and I don't criticize myself anymore for mistakes, or even for tilting. Now if I make a mistake or tilt, I just reflect on it and identify all the factors—poker or mental—that caused it. I know I'm never going to be mistake-free, and I don't want to say I am tilt-free either, because I'm not. But it's amazing how differently I carry myself now in poker. Ever since our fourth lesson, a lot of weight has been gone. I still feel pressure, but it's never overwhelming, and I take a healthier, more relaxed approach to the game."

Moving Up in Stakes

Look out for entitlement tilt when moving up in stakes. Players often feel entitled to win because they were winners at the stakes below. As a result, they are often quick to think the regulars at the next limit are terrible. Avoid making these errors. They create false confidence and will damage your potential success at that limit and your long-term success in poker.

REVENGE TILT

Revenge is common in everyday life, so it's no surprise it also is common in poker. And, just as in life, the long-term consequences of revenge at the poker table often outweigh the short-term satisfaction of achieving it. Of course, the consequences aren't in the front of your mind when you play back at constant 3-betting, berate your opponent, or hunt down a hit-and-runner. You want revenge. You want to get back at them. You want them to feel your pain. You want to humiliate them for what they just did, and like Tony Montana in *Scarface,* that piercing look in your eyes says you want revenge.

Reacting this way is especially surprising to players who generally don't seek revenge outside of poker. Typically, they don't feel that vengeful towards someone, so wanting to destroy an opponent at the poker table is a bit shocking. Something about poker brings out a vengeful side. For some players, the reason they seek revenge in poker and not in life is that poker pushes them in a way life does not. For other players, who in life tend to keep their anger in, poker is a place where they can finally push back.

Revenge is not irrational. It has a history of helping to create laws, unwritten codes of the street,[5] and the unwritten rules that you define as acceptable and unacceptable in poker. Revenge doesn't exist when another player's actions are acceptable to you. When opponents treat you with

---

5   Dr. Michael McCullough, PhD, University of Miami; The *New York Times,* July 27, 2004, Payback Time: Why Revenge Tastes So Sweet, by Benedict Carey.

respect, don't try to outplay you, or keep playing as long as you want them to, there's no reason to be angry. According to your laws of poker, that's what's supposed to happen. As long as they do what you say, there's no reason for revenge.

Your opponents don't care about your rules. They play by their own rules and rules of the game. This means the underlying problem causing revenge tilt is with you—not with them. Even though they hit and ran, their constant aggression forced you to take a stand, or their annoying comments made you want to choke them out, they are not the actual problem (unless they're actually breaking poker room rules or the law). Aside from extreme situations, whenever you seek revenge for the things players do to set you off, your anger is a signal that indicates there's a flaw in your mental game.

To start uncovering these flaws, make a list of the triggers that spark revenge. Here are a few common ones:

- Having your money taken.
- Being slighted or not shown enough respect.
- Constantly being 3-bet.
- Feeling like you're getting run over.
- Another player trying to make you look stupid.
- Your opponent thinking he is better than you.
- Something about them just pisses you off.
- Feeling as if your opponent is in your head and knows exactly what you're doing.
- A player with whom you have history.

Injustice tilt tends to be anger toward poker and variance, whereas revenge tilt targets specific players. You may also notice that revenge tilt is more intense when playing Heads Up.

Revenge in poker is only sweet when you use your anger as fuel to play well. Otherwise, it's a losing strategy in the long run. While you may already know that, you need to know it well enough to prevent your game from being hijacked by the desire to exact revenge. As with all the other causes of tilt, knowing the problem doesn't mean you automatically know the solution. Now that you've identified what sets off your revenge tilt, the next step is to understand the reason(s) you seek revenge, and then you can begin to resolve the flaw in that reasoning.

Think about the last time you sought revenge, or a time when that desire was especially strong. What was your underlying motive for revenge? What did you want? What were you trying to accomplish with your actions? Here are some answers to those questions:

- "I want to show them who's better."
- "I want them to feel my pain."
- "I don't want them thinking they're better than me."
- "I don't want to get owned."
- "I'm protecting my bankroll."
- "I want to hurt them."

While each of these and other motives have unique details, which are discussed in the upcoming sections, the overall reason you seek revenge is control.

Vengeance is rooted in a desire to show the other players that you have control of the situation, they don't. You're letting them know they're not going to outplay you, they're not going to disrespect you, and they're not getting away with your money. Nor can they push you around anymore, or try to run you over. You're taking back control and retaliating for the harm they caused.

In actuality, trying to take control of the situation in the way that you do, shows that you're out of control. Ultimately, you have no control of your opponents. You don't get to decide how long they play, how they play, what they say, or whether they get your message. Like you, they are motivated by their own interests. But if your interest is in controlling them, then you have less focus and energy devoted to controlling your game. Playing poorly because of vengeful actions proves you're in far less control of the outcome.

The solution to revenge tilt is to use your anger as a way to:

1. Identify specific situations where you are giving up control of your game.
2. Resolve the flawed reasons why you give up control.
3. Improve the technical poker mistakes you tend to make at this time.

No Respect

Being disrespected by another player is often seen as a cue to beat some respect into them. While there are hundreds of reasons to feel disrespected—many of which are legitimate—the bottom line is that you have no control over what other players think of you or your game. That doesn't make what they say right, cordial, or respectful; it just means you can't control what comes out of their mouths.

Look at it from their perspective. It's not personal. They are trying to do the same thing: win. How they try to win is not up to you, just as they can't decide how you play. If what they say or do pisses you off and causes you to tilt, they win on another level. Anger can be a destructive force, but you can also harness that power and use it as fuel to become a stronger player. The key is using your anger to motivate you to play better and work harder off the table, rather than trying to control how they play.

Michael Jordan famously said in his Hall of Fame induction speech that he was motivated by all the people who thought he couldn't succeed, most notably, his high school basketball coach who cut him and the sportswriters who doubted he could win an NBA championship. Jordan even took subtle (perhaps unintended) slights by other players as disrespect, so he could have extra motivation to beat them on the court. Is this the purest form of motivation? No, but it worked for him. If you become a better player, win more money, and achieve more success in poker by using revenge to fuel your motivation, it can't be that bad. Ideal? No. Bad? Hell no.

When you avenge being disrespected, be sure to recognize the work you put into your game. It's easy to ignore the steps you took to improve your game when the satisfaction from successfully achieving revenge is focused on your opponents. They may have motivated you, but you did the work, so enjoy it. You earned it.

 USE YOUR ANGER AS FUEL TO PLAY BETTER THAN EVER.

Facing Constant Aggression

Some players get tilted by an opponent's aggressive action. It feels like their game is under attack when constantly being 3-bet and c-bet, or their opponents play more than 50% of hands and put them in a lot of difficult spots. While anger is partially related to other causes of revenge tilt, it also protects weaknesses in your game. Defending your game with revenge can happen simply by lacking enough experience or tactical knowledge to handle constant aggression. Once you know how to profitably play these situations, your frustration goes away. *On page 24 a client describes how that happened for him.*

If fixing the weaknesses in your game that are exposed by revenge tilt doesn't eliminate your revenge tilt, there are other reasons for it.

IT ONLY SEEMS AS IF THEY ARE ALL PLAYING BACK AT YOU—STAY IN CONTROL AND PLAY YOUR GAME. THAT'S ALL YOU CAN DO.

Player with History

Many players, in particular those at high stakes and who live in areas where the player pool is small, have a player with whom they have "history." This poker nemesis is someone who always seems to outplay you, get lucky against you, or act like a complete ass when they win. Just hearing this person's name gets you angry, let alone having to sit at the table with them. At this point, beating them has become about much more than just money.

Keep in mind, this kind of revenge tilt doesn't have to be obvious to the other player or anyone else to be a problem for you. Keeping your anger hidden as much as possible—especially in live games—is a good strategy. The problem is that internally tilting can still affect your play. It may not cause you to start spewing, but if you're in a tough game, the subtle effects can negatively impact your decision making.

This type of revenge tilt is a form of accumulated tilt; you can't have it toward someone you're playing against for the first time. The problem you have with this player has built up over time. Each time you play, the action means so much more because of that history. The bad blood that's formed over time may be so strong that you get pissed off just by hearing their name or thinking about them. If that's true, when you play them your anger is intense, even if days, weeks, or even years pass. When you sit across from them, the history between you is a huge part of the action.

Use the following advice to take advantage of the history with this player:

1. *Use your history, rather than having it control you.*
   To do that, start by finding out why you hate this player so much. What is it about them or the action between you that pisses you

off? Have they gotten lucky and think they're better than you? Are they actually better, and you hate them for it? Are they a rival who always seems to get the better of you? Is it something about them personally (the way they talk, act, or dress)? Whatever the reason, recognizing why they get under your skin is key to working through your revenge tilt, because it then gives you a chance to figure out what you're trying to control.

2. **Expect your anger to be intense.** When injecting logic, you're essentially going to be fighting yourself to stay in control. The battle is no longer just between you and the player you want to destroy. You also have to fight to keep your anger from causing you to play badly.

   Your anger towards them may never go away completely, but that's not a bad thing. As long as you can keep it below your tilt threshold, you can use whatever anger remains to fuel your focus and play great. Revenge is great motivation to play at your best, as long as you remain in control of it.

3. **They're going to try and get under your skin.** If they're used to seeing you blow up, but you're controlling your game more, they may see that as a challenge to try harder to piss you off. It's the game within the game. Be ready to win that too.

4. **Look closely at your prior action.** In addition to looking for weaknesses in their game, consider how you can use their past knowledge about your tilt to your advantage. This only works if you're able to remain in control and avoid tilt.

5. *The steps on page 66 can help resolve the accumulated emotion surrounding your past history with them.*

6. *Review the client story on page 133.*

INJECTING LOGIC

IF YOU LOSE CONTROL, THEN YOUR NEMESIS REALLY WINS.

Regaining Confidence

Getting crushed by an opponent, or when variance makes it seem that way, can make you fight back by playing sub-optimally. Sometimes it happens so subtly that the first thing you notice is being in the middle of a fight trying to regain control of the action. Often, you're also fighting to regain your confidence.

When getting outplayed and being totally owned by your opponent, it can feel as if they've taken your confidence along with your chips. You take a stand. You're not going to get run over. You force the action trying to exact revenge for them even thinking they can toy with you. You recklessly 3-bet in the hope you can show down a bluff or try to make ludicrous hero calls. Nothing you do works, it just causes you to lose more. On the surface you are trying to play back at them to show that you're the better player. But you're also trying to prove that to yourself.

It's to your advantage when your opponent misinterprets your ability. The only logical reason you'd want to prove to them that they can't run you over is because you need to prove that to yourself.

This confidence problem happens when you lack the ability to recognize your skill, your opponent's skill, and variance. When you know your edge in the game, there's no reason for you to try outplaying your opponent in a vengeful way. Developing these skills may not solve your problems with revenge tilt, but they are important pieces of the puzzle. *See page 211 for more.*

Taking Your Money

When it feels as if the money that's been won off of you was stolen, revenge tilt busts out like a debt collector ready to break some kneecaps.

You want your money back now! You can't wait to get into a hand with them. Your focus fixates on them. You don't let them out of your sight. God help them if they leave the table, because you will hunt them down until you win your money back.

While the intensity of each player's tilt varies, the common denominator is money. What is it about the money you lost that sends you into a blind rage? Money always represents something more than just its actual value, so what does it represent to you? Is it competition, since money is the way to keep score in poker? Do you hate losing? Money can be connected to goals, accomplishment, status in the game, or the real need to pay the bills and live. Money serves many purposes. The reason(s) you tilt to protect losing money is the weakness to address.

When you lose money, you perceive that revenge protects you from being viewed as a losing player, from losing the money you need to pay bills, or from falling below your expectations. Revenge is purposeful—it's just misguided. Instead of actually preventing yourself from losing money, you may lose more of it. As long as you can maintain your edge in the game, especially at times when revenge tilt destroys it, the money will come back; just maybe not from the same player.

The correction to this type of revenge tilt is not just to numb the anger that is protecting your money. That short term solution doesn't address the underlying cause of your anger, so you need to:

1. **Be less results-oriented.** Focusing more on money than how well you're playing puts a lot of pressure on your mental game when you lose. Instead, focus more on the quality of your play, so losing money will matter less in the short run. *To improve the skill of recognizing the quality of your skill, go to page 212.*

2. **View money as an investment in your edge.** Your investment isn't going to yield a return every time you play poker. *For more, go to page 112.*

3. *Review page 109 to understand more about what money represents to you.*

Enacting Revenge

Losing is painful. You probably hate it. You may even hate the players you lose to. Over time, names no longer matter, you just hate whoever beats you and want them to feel your pain. Intense as that sounds, often the pain you feel when losing is what forms the roots of revenge.

The battle for supremacy at the table is also a battle for who is going to feel the pain of losing and who will feel the satisfaction of victory. Essentially, revenge tilt is a defensive strategy designed to protect you from feeling the pain of losing.

Except the reality is not everyone experiences losing in the same way as you. Many of the players that you want to inflict pain on aren't going to feel it because losing doesn't bother them as much as it bothers you. If you want to resolve this type of revenge tilt, you need to reduce the amount of pain you feel when losing. *The steps outlined in hate-losing tilt beginning on page 108 can help.*

Your Soul Owned

You have to look at the reverse side of revenge in order to complete the picture of why you seek it: How you feel when running over another player.

Does it feel as if you're in complete control? As if you own their soul? If so, how intense are those positive emotions associated with power and control?

Since this type of revenge tilt can seem odd, you may not think you have it at first. Look closely at the intent behind your anger to find out if deep down you believe you have the ability to own another player's game and work them like a puppet master.

It's not possible to be in control of another player's game, but it makes sense why it can appear that way: Deep understanding mimics control. When you understand a player's game better than they do, you basically know how to exploit their weaknesses and stay at least a step ahead of their adjustments. They have no way to beat you. You are in complete control of the match or the action. The only way you'll lose is because of variance. While you're in complete control of the action, that doesn't mean you control them, it means you understand their game. Plus, you're probably playing really well and feeling great about your game. Both of these factors add to a sense of being in complete control; and you also might be running well. Believing you control another player's game makes sense for these reasons; they just happen to be flawed.

Revenge comes into the picture because losing makes it appear as if your opponent owns you. If you believe you can own another player, that means you also believe someone can own you. Revenge tilt is your way of protecting against that happening.

DESPERATION TILT

Desperation is a feeling that can be hard to recognize. Spotting it requires looking closely at the intent behind actions such as trying to get unstuck, chasing losses, playing outside your bankroll, raising every hand, constantly checking results, forcing action, jumping up in stakes, playing monster long sessions, and rapidly reloading. What makes them acts of desperation is the intent or urge to do everything possible to win immediately, get even, or avoid taking a loss.

In a flash, you can wake up having spewed off a ton of money, grinding for 16 hours straight, or worse. Avoiding the urge to do everything to win is tough because it just gets stronger and stronger the more you lose. It's an itch you *have* to scratch, so walking away from poker becomes increasingly harder to do. Winning, it seems, is the only thing that makes the itch go away. You get some relief from desperation if you're able to squeeze out a victory or at least avoid a big loss, but it's only temporary.

Once losses pile up again, desperation comes back as though it was never gone. Actually it never left, it was just hiding.

Much like a person addicted to drugs will do anything to score their next fix, a poker player desperate to win their money back will do almost anything to win. Actually that's not true; they won't do *anything*. The distinction between what they will and will not do determines whether they have a performance issue or a gambling problem.

All the issues described in this book exist along a spectrum of intensity. Poker players with mild enough forms of desperation tilt can use the advice in this section to make solid improvement. Others could benefit from professional help. There's a line for each player between a performance issue and a gambling problem. If desperation tilt is a problem for you, deciding which side of the line you're on is a judgment call. Can you remain in enough control when this problem is at its worst, and afford any personal and financial losses that may happen while working on this problem yourself? Or, do you need the help of a psychologist who specializes in gambling problems?

Desperation tilt is a slippery slope that takes hard work to prevent. When it happens to a skilled player, it's hard to comprehend afterwards just how badly they played. The gap between how they play normally and when desperation tilting is so wide, it can seem as if they're possessed by a demon. Without knowing why it happens, it's impossible to prevent. This uncertainty only adds more emotional pain to an issue barely comprehensible already.

Desperation tilt is a form of accumulated tilt. The intensity of the anger that shows up when trying to get unstuck is so strong that it very quickly takes over your mind. Old emotion floods the mind and drowns it in so much anger that your reaction to the situation is beyond reason. You do things that don't make sense and tilt even more because of how irrational you seem to be.

If this pattern has been going on for a while, the anger that floods your mind has been building up for years. Even if it's only recently become severe in poker, working away from the table is mandatory to build up the mental muscle needed to make it a fair fight. Accumulated tilt is the real wild card with this type of tilt. The more you've accumulated, the harder it is to keep yourself thinking and thus maintain control. If you try to take desperation tilt head-on without serious preparation, you have little to no chance of correcting it. The accumulated anger quickly overwhelms your mind and you play terribly. Rather than showing up unprepared, work away from the action with a sense of urgency as if your poker life depends on it. It does.

WHEN LOSING FEELS GOOD

Sometimes the urge to win is so strong, losing feels good. Admitting you want to lose sounds a bit crazy, but it happens often enough to regular people that it doesn't necessarily mean you're nuts. Losing can feel good for a number of logical reasons. It gets the pain over with quickly, you can control it, and it can be a relief from the pressure to win. Players with desperation tilt often get stuck trying to figure out why they want to lose. That uncertainty adds more frustration (the tilt of tilt) and ultimately makes desperation tilt more likely to happen again.

Desperation tilt is caused by underlying issues already covered in this chapter. Desperation tilt is like a trap door that lies beneath each type of tilt—most commonly hate-losing tilt—waiting to drag you down into poker hell. Poker players with desperation tilt hate walking away from the table stuck, and simply don't want to end a session down money no matter how long it takes to win. The longer and deeper the losses get, the worse they play, the stronger the anger becomes, and the more likely they'll be to do something drastic such as jumping up in stakes, shoving any hand, or straddling every big blind.

While the other types of tilt can lead to desperation tilt, you may not be sure which one causes you to become desperate yet. That's fine. The first goal is to prevent desperation tilt, since it can cause major damage to your bank-roll, confidence, and motivation. The primary goal of this section is to help you prevent that from happening. Start with the standard strategy provided below. Then, after paying closer attention to your triggers and signs of tilt, eventually you'll identify the type of tilt that's causing desperation.

Non-negotiable Strategy

Follow all or the majority of these steps to prevent desperation tilt from destroying your game:

1. **Have a sense of urgency.** It's a major mistake to take desperation tilt or the steps to correct it too causally. If you think that you'll wake up one day to the problem being gone, you're dreaming and gambling with your mental game. For every player who stops cold turkey, like a smoker who one day quits and never smokes again, there are many more who fail trying. If you want your tilt problem to improve, it has to be your top priority.

2. **Write a tilt profile.** Be sure to detail the early signs that tilt is rising, what may be triggering your tilt, and the first poker mistakes you make. Study your profile often and before you play. Add new details when you find them. *For more, see page 76.*

   One of the major reasons you have trouble controlling tilt is the early warning signs aren't even on your radar. In order to have a chance at stopping tilt you *have* to be able to spot the signs when your anger starts rising.

3. **Set strict stop/loss.** Sure, you've probably set these before and blown through them, but that doesn't make it a bad strategy. It's unlikely you combined a stop/loss with other steps to prevent tilt, or realized how important it is to maintain conscious control of your emotions.

4. **Take regular breaks or use a timer.** Maintaining emotional control throughout the session is critical. If anger starts taking over your ability to think, you're far more likely to succumb to the intense accumulated tilt that follows close behind. While this strategy may keep you from playing your best, it's far better than the alternative. *See page 53 for specific details.*

5. **Review your emergency response.** Before every session, review your strategy to prevent desperation tilt as if rehearsing for an emergency. This keeps all the details of your plan fresh in your mind, so you're ready to take emergency action.

6. **Take aggressive action toward the early signs of tilt.** Once you spot the signs of tilt, work hard to control your anger by implementing each part of your strategy.

7. **Recognize small steps forward.** Recognizing sessions where you make progress with tilt gives you a boost in confidence to keep you working hard. Remember, increased recognition or awareness of tilt, not control of tilt, can often be the first step. Desperation tilt is a major problem, and eliminating it takes sustained effort over a long period of time. When small improvements go unnoticed, you might abandon a strategy that's actually working. *For more on tracking improvement, go to page 64.*

8. **After identifying the type(s) of tilt that leads to desperation, resolve it using the mental hand history.** Taking these steps reduces the amount of anger that shows up when triggered, which makes it easier to implement any of the previous seven steps. *The mental hand history is on page 61.*

9. **Better understand the learning process.** A contributing cause of desperation tilt is inaccurate assumptions about learning. Review chapter 2 so you know what to expect.

10.Develop stable confidence by reading chapter 8.
Players with stable confidence don't have desperation tilt.

USING TILT TO IMPROVE YOUR PLAY

In the beginning of this chapter, tilt was introduced as something that could benefit your game. Tilting is far from an ideal way to improve, but when it's a real part of your game, make use of what it gives you rather than just having it abuse you. Here's a quick refresher on how that's possible.

When anger becomes too intense and crosses your threshold, your brain malfunctions. Higher brain functions—such as decision making, perception, and emotional control—begin shutting down. You make terrible decisions because you aren't thinking straight. According to the ALM, losing your ability to think means you've lost the information that is currently in the process of being learned: Conscious Competence. What's left are the skills or knowledge in your game that you've mastered: Unconscious Competence. That includes the solid parts of your game that you want to keep, and the weak parts that need to improve. Everything that did not show up you simply have not learned or mastered yet, and is still in the process of being learned.

When analyzing the quality of your play on tilt, consider these three categories:

1. Core knowledge that is solid and is your mastered strength.
2. Core knowledge that is outdated, old, and is your greatest weakness (a.k.a., bad habits).
3. Knowledge in the process of being learned.

Recognizing the mastered strengths in your game is key for three reasons:

1. You identify areas you never have to work on again.

2. You create a balanced perspective of your game.

3. You recognize the limit to how badly you can play. Your game can't fall into some black hole that can deteriorate into complete oblivion. These strengths are guaranteed to show up no matter how tilted you become.

Recognizing your greatest weaknesses is important because these are the easiest parts of your game to correct. While the reality of your game at its worst can be harsh to accept, the good news is that when you correct these mistakes you have less to think about. Since the corrections to your weaknesses haven't been mastered, they require thought. When you master the corrections to the level of Unconscious Competence, you free up mental space to take your game to an even higher level. *See page 16 for more.*

The best way to start correcting your greatest weaknesses is by making a list of them, along with the corrections to each one and reviewing it before you play. Then, while playing, do everything you can to make those corrections at times when you recognize anger rising. Since these weaknesses are so basic compared to your strengths, they don't require much thought, which means they'll be easy to correct the next time you're on tilt. However, you still must treat them as a priority. The correction to a weakness is only mastered when you have proven you can correct it while tilting. That means you can take it off your list and replace it with your next greatest weakness. Remember, no matter how good you become, you'll always have weaknesses. *Go to page 122, for a slightly more advanced way of using tilt to analyze your game.*

Keeping Records

When using the strategy above, write out your list of notes and keep them organized by date. It doesn't take long, and is valuable for these two reasons:

1. Writing out your notes makes each weakness more real, and more likely to stand out and be corrected when tilting. While the mistakes you make on tilt are obvious afterward, they need to be obvious when it matters most: before you act. Writing them down speeds that up that process.

2. As you continue to write out your weaknesses over time, you create a paper trail that allows you to prove you're improving as a player. When making progress with tilt, the intensity of your anger may seem the same but your game may have improved. Your notes give you a way to compare your current worst to your previous worst months ago, and prove whether the back end of your game improved.

Remember, improvement happens in two ways: Your best gets better and your worst gets better. Using the steps above allows you to prove if your worst is improving, which indicates you're doing the right things. This way, the next time you tilt, you have a small positive to take away at a time when you would have previously only seen negatives.

It's also possible that no improvements have been made. Here are a few reasons:

- The cause of your tilt is not resolved.
- Tilt is more severe than at any other time since you started keeping records.
- Your approach to improving isn't working. Review chapters 2, 3, and 4.

6

F E A R

IN A POKER WORLD WHERE everything short of playing your best is called tilt, players barely notice anxiety and fear. Defining tilt as just being caused by anger allows fear to emerge as a real contributor to mental game problems. Fear was there all along, but unless you had the ability to spot it, it's likely you'd miss its role in causing problems in your game. Many players do. You may not realize that fear can be the cause of struggling to think clearly, constantly checking past hands for mistakes, or why you lack the energy to play.

While you may not experience fear in a big way, it may show up more subtly in one of the following ways:

- Your mind goes blank in big pots.
- You feel rushed for no apparent reason.
- You constantly replay previous hands in your mind.
- You constantly check results, the cashier, or your stack size.
- You play poker only when you're feeling perfect, so you don't play much.
- Your mind races and you can't stop thinking.

- You constantly second-guess decisions.
- You avoid high-variance plays that you know are the right decision.
- You take extra time over a tough decision, but still are not thinking about anything except, "What the hell do I do?"
- You feel overwhelmed about learning the game.
- You regularly lose your train of thought in a hand.
- You're reluctant to move up in stakes.
- You struggle sleeping after bad sessions.

The Nature of Fear

Fear is an accumulation of anxiety.

Anxiety is an accumulation of doubt or uncertainty.

Uncertainty is essentially a question you don't have the answer for, or don't have enough experience to prove the answer you already have is correct. When these questions are unanswered or unproven, doubt lingers and eventually accumulates into anxiety. If this goes on long enough, it turns into fear. As with other emotions, fear exists along a spectrum, only it begins as a question.

By digging into your fear, you can pull out the questions that are unanswered or unproven. Uncovering the questions underlying your fear is important because they indicate what you want to know at a deeper level. The following are examples of common questions poker players have:

- "If I can't beat the fish, how can I ever be successful?"
- "What will I do if online poker goes away, or the games dry up?"
- "Is this the right decision here?"
- "How could I have been so stupid?"

- "When is the bad run going to end?"
- "Why does this always happen to me?"
- "Why can't I ever play well when I move up in stakes?"
- "Will I ever be able to reach my potential?"
- "Will I make it as a pro?"
- "What will I do if I can't make it as a pro?"
- "Can I handle another sickening downswing?"
- "Will I wake up one day not being able to win at poker?"

Sometimes these questions linger in a player's mind without being answered, while at other times they're answered automatically with responses such as, "It's because I'm stupid that I make these mistakes," "I'll never be successful if I can't beat the fish," "The bad run is never going to end," or "It's because I'm just not a good enough player to ever make it as a pro." These answers perpetuate fear.

It may seem overly simplistic to reduce fear down to a question, but think about it logically. When you have certainty, there's nothing to fear. This is why people who have certainty display confidence, even when they're wrong.

If you were 100% sure that online poker was going to be legalized and would lead to a second poker boom, it would be illogical to worry about it going away. If you were 100% sure that your bad run was going to end in 10,000 hands, you wouldn't think twice about sitting down to play those 10,000 hands as quickly as possible. As simple as it sounds, certainty is the antidote to fear.

Unpredictability or uncertainty alone does not create anxiety—just as anger alone does not create tilt. To reach that level of intensity requires underlying flaws in how you're approaching and learning poker. The end goal is not to eliminate uncertainty; it's to correct the underlying flaws in your logic that force you to *need* certainty when you really can't have it yet. Without uncertainty, there is no risk. Without risk, there is nothing to gain in poker, no edge to create, and no profit to be made.

BARRY'S TAKE

Be Fearless Like Ivey

Players often have a desire to be fearless, just like how they perceive Phil Ivey—an entity devoid of all fear with the ability to invoke fear in others. Trying to be fearless like Ivey without actually removing the very real fears you have is a results-oriented way of thinking about the mental game. You see the sum of his mental game parts, but not how he got there. It's no different than wanting to have as much money or to be as good of a player. You see the end result and think it can be yours without actually earning it. Unfortunately, the mind is powerful enough to convince you that it's possible, but not powerful enough to instantly make it a reality.

Incomplete Information

You no doubt have heard poker referred to as a game of incomplete information. The skill in poker comes from creating certainty where there were previously unknowns. You have no idea what hole cards your opponent has been dealt, but you have the ability to put them on ranges, retrace previous hands with them, and pick up on their tells to fill in that missing information. You don't know the strength of your opponent after playing one hand with them; but if you regularly watch training videos, post on forums, and work on your game, you can learn how to quickly assess their game.

Hypothetically, let's say there are 10 technical unknowns in any given poker hand. A fish can only fill in one or two of the unknown variables in a hand, whereas a professional player can fill in seven. A professional's edge comes from their ability to create certainty where weaker players can't. In other words, they have an informational advantage.

A player is a mental game fish when they lack the proficiency to fill in enough of the unknown variables. Hypothetically, let's also say that there are 10 technical unknown variables within a mental game issue. Players with anxiety or fear problems typically have the skill to fill in one or two, but believe they have the skill to fill in seven. Since they believe they *should* be able to figure it out, they scour their mind for the answer. When there's no answer to be found, their thinking moves faster and eventually races to desperately fill in the unknown variables. They constantly check the cashier, but don't know why; their mind goes blank when playing $5/$10, but they can't figure out why it doesn't happen at lower stakes; or they rush decisions in big pots, but can't figure out how to slow down.

Trying to fill in more unknowns than your mental game skill allows is just like trying to out-level a superior player. Your mind outthinks itself and your results are even worse than if you stuck to what you know. Fortunately, a player fills the unknown variables in the mental game by developing skill in the same way as in the game itself; only the details differ.

Fuel to Perform
"If you aren't feeling pressure on the 1st tee of a major golf tournament, you aren't alive." — Overheard on the PGA Tour.

While fear causes a host of problems, when experienced at low levels, it can be a major source of fuel for you to perform at your highest level and get into the zone. In pressure situations, it's common to feel anxious, nervous, excited, amped, or jacked up. However you describe it, having emotion and adrenaline pumping through your body primes your senses to pick up on details you can't see normally. It's because you're picking up on those details that it feels as if the action just flows through you, time seems to slow down, and you just *know* what your opponent is holding. You're in the zone, thanks to your nerves.

In poker, as in sports, business, and other performance arenas, the ability to thrive under pressure previously gave people a distinct competitive advantage. It's one that kept them from being naturally selected out of the game—until psychology and sport psychology gave people who struggled to perform under pressure a formal way to learn this previously unattainable skill. These people may have been equally, if not more talented, but without the ability to perform under pressure, they couldn't achieve a level of success equal to their talent.

For poker players who lack the ability to perform under pressure, this chapter intends to level the playing field. When addressing issues of fear, the goal is to identify and break down the underlying flaws in your mental game that turn your questions into fear. One example of such a flaw is the belief that feeling anxious or fearful means you'll perform poorly. When you experienced normal nerves at the table, your mind couldn't answer the questions: "Why do I feel this way?" and "What does feeling this way mean for my performance?" Your inability to answer these questions created more anxiety, which shut down your mind and made it more likely for you to fail. Over time, you associated anxiety with failing, so you learned that anxiety was inherently bad. Since you learned how to fear your nerves, you can also learn how to use them to play your best poker.

Here are a couple of other benefits that fear or pressure provides:

1. Just like tilt, anxiety exposes underlying weaknesses in how you technically play poker and approach the mental game. Basically, it helps you identify what you need to improve.
2. Pressure is critical for learning. When your nerves are amped up to the top of the performance curve, you become a learning machine that's capable of picking up on subtle details in the action that you normally couldn't see.

By embracing anxiety, you're in a great position to capitalize on it.

FEAR PROFILE

Before addressing your fears directly, first you need to recognize and understand them better. The best way is to identify your patterns of doubt, anxiety, and fear. Here are a few questions to get you started:

- What are the situations that typically provoke doubt, anxiety, or fear?
- What are your earliest signs of fear?
- Do you struggle with any of the things listed on *page 155* or have any of the questions listed on *page 156*? Can you describe them in more detail?
- Can you identify the point when anxiety goes from helping you perform to being excessive and causing problems?
- How do you experience anxiety? (Heart pounding, sweating, nausea, dry mouth, foot or hand tapping, etc.)

When analyzing your pattern, think about the presence of the five common symptoms of fear described below. Poker players often view these as being inherently negative and bad for their game. They're not. They are associated with the underlying flaw(s) causing your fear. When you understand them, you're a step closer to removing them and solving your problems with anxiety and fear.

1. Overthinking

Fear causes your mind to race, to go around in circles, and to obsess over one thing. This happens because your mind can't find the answer to your underlying question. The antidote to fear is certainty, so the mind does everything it can to find an answer. When really desperate to find an answer, the mind continues until it's exhausted or gets distracted.

Since the mind is limited to a finite number of things it can think about at one time, write down your thoughts. Writing down what you're worried about makes it easier to figure out the underlying question you're trying to answer. Once you've identified the question, write out the answer.

Overthinking creates confusion and clutter in your mind. A cluttered mind is like a cluttered desk; it's difficult to find what you're looking for. Writing helps you to clear out the clutter and use your mind more efficiently to find answers.

2. Not Trusting Your Gut

You know the right play, but go against it. Why? It's because you don't trust the answer your gut spits out. This leads us to ask, "What the hell is the gut?" If you don't know what the gut is, it makes sense why you wouldn't trust it. Essentially, the gut is skills at the level of Unconscious Competence reacting to the situation with an answer. It's the mental version of an athletic reaction in sports.

One example of this is when a basketball player driving to the basket instantly adjusts the placement of the ball in his hand to avoid a defender's attempt to cut him off. There's no thinking in this athletic move, it's a purely instinctive reaction. The same is true on a mental level; the gut doesn't think to come up with the answer, the answer comes automatically.

BARRY'S TAKE

Feel Players

You often hear about "feel players." These are players who seem to have some mystifying soul-reading ability, but in reality, they're just using their skills trained to the level of Unconscious Competence really well.

Mental reactions, just like athletic ones, happen thanks to deeply ingrained skill. If you don't trust your gut, you don't trust all the work you've put into learning the game. When your gut is right, you learn it's something you can trust and use as a part of your decision making. However, sometimes your training is old or flawed, so your gut is wrong. When that happens, it means you've found a weakness in your knowledge base to correct. Once you correct that weakness, your game becomes even more solid because your gut is more accurate.

3. Second-guessing

While you're playing, the urge to know the correct decision in hands where you lost or made a mistake can be so strong that you replay them repeatedly in your mind or review the actual hand history. You've made a move, lost the hand, and now you question it. You wonder if it was wrong. There are so many times when the decision is close, and not knowing if it was right or wrong can be agonizing.

Second-guessing means you have doubts or questions about a decision after you make it. Often, this is fueled by a desire to make sure you don't lose more or make more mistakes. However, being distracted by previous hands makes both more likely to happen. The best thing to do is to take a quick note and then revisit the hand after you're done playing.

4. Performance Anxiety

Playing poker is a test to prove what you know. Players with performance anxiety put so much pressure on themselves to make the correct decision that they end up overthinking, not trusting their gut, and second-guessing their decisions. Unfortunately, these actions make them play worse, and make it harder for them to access all of their poker knowledge.

Test your game when you play poker instead of overthinking, not trusting your gut, or second-guessing your decisions. Then you can more accurately evaluate the strengths and weaknesses in your game so you know specifically what needs to improve. This way, you're better prepared to take the next test.

5. Negative Future

Additional fear is created by anticipating the fear you will have about things that could happen in the future. This fear of fear causes players to make mistakes, delay starting a session, avoid high-variance plays, and play less poker overall. What creates this additional fear is the belief that what is predicted to happen in the future *will* happen. They don't just *think* they're going to play badly and lose, they *know* it.

Poker players make shitty psychics. They can't predict the future. What they imagine happening in the future is a prediction, not what will actually happen. Believing the prediction will become a reality adds more fear, which prevents a player from thinking clearly. Consequently, losing, making mistakes, and a bad run become more likely—and what was previously feared becomes a reality. Preparation, injecting logic while playing, and the writing exercises described in the next section, all make it less likely that your predicted negative future will become a reality.

GENERAL STRATEGY FOR RESOLVING FEAR

Begin resolving your fear by writing down the thoughts and underlying questions surrounding it. Externalizing what's on your mind allows you to look at the details of your fear more objectively. Plus, writing is one of the quickest ways to make rapid progress. It clears your mind so it's easier to think through decisions while you're playing. Starting on the next page are two writing exercises that you can use to make efficient progress toward resolving your fear. *For more details about why writing is effective, see page 65.*

Playing Out the Fear

What's the worst that could happen? This is a common question asked by people trying to help someone get over their fear. This strategy takes the essence of that question a step further.

Start by taking the thing you're fearful of, and writing down the answer to the question, "What's the worst that could happen?" Then ask follow-up questions, such as "Why is that bad?"; "What would happen?"; "What would you do?"; "How would you feel?"; "What's the solution?" Answering these questions helps you better understand what's causing your fear. Then, directly address your fear by breaking down the underlying flaw, finding something productive to do, and thinking better overall.

Here's an example of how you can "play out the fear" of moving up in stakes in writing:

> What's the worst thing that would happen if you moved up in stakes and had a downswing? *"I would lose money and confidence."*
>
> What would that do to you? *"I would have to drop back down and build my way back up."*
>
> How would that feel? *"It would suck, of course; I've been grinding for a while and just can't seem to break through. I can't seem to figure it out."*
>
> Have you done everything you can to figure it out? *"I've done a lot. Maybe there's more, I don't know. I'm just not sure what I could do."*
>
> How can you find out? *"I could ask around. I have a few poker friends who could probably help. I've posted on forums a few times; I could do that, maybe hire a coach."*

Why does it suck to go back to the grind at lower stakes? *"I just want things to be easier and not have to go through these constant ups and downs. It's so damn frustrating. I just freak out whenever I play higher."*

What do you freak out about? *"I don't know; I guess because I've failed so many times my brain locks up and I play like a donkey. I just want to make it so badly."*

How can you make it more likely that you'll succeed? *"Probably by putting in more work. I tend to blow it off when things aren't going well and I just really need to be more consistent with it. It may not be fun, but it's the only way."*

There's more to this problem, but at this point you've figured out a productive step to take: do more work, especially when you don't want to. This solution alone isn't going to eliminate the uncertainty or even all the fear of moving up, but it's a step in the right direction.

Part of what's causing the fear in this example is a desire for success at higher stakes to come easily and some uncertainty about how to improve. This technique helps to dig through the layers of fear to find the cause of fear and a way to resolve it. Too often, players play into their fear, and avoid moving up. The overall goal is to break through the fear so it no longer holds you back.

Answering Questions

When questions go unanswered, they stew in the back of your mind and subtly undermine your effort to play solid poker. The longer they go unanswered, the more havoc they create. The first step in this strategy is to state the uncertainty you have in your game in the form of a question. For example:

- "What if I'm not good enough?"
- "What if I can't make it?"

- "If I can't beat this guy, how can I ever beat regulars at the next limit?"

The second step is to reword questions about the future that can't be answered yet. Here are a couple good examples:

- "When is the bad run going to end?" Since you can't know that, the better question is, "What do I need to do to improve how I handle running bad?"
- "Can I make it as a pro?" The better question is, "What do I need to do to give myself the best chance to make it as a pro?"

The third step is to answer each question. Too often, players ignore their questions and think they're stupid or illogical, when really they're legitimate and reasonable questions to ask. By answering them, you develop the certainty needed to resolve your fear. You can't eliminate uncertainty in poker, but you can eliminate fear. Answering the legitimate questions in your game helps you to accomplish this.

For both writing exercises, if the answers don't come immediately, it's better to be accurate and go slower rather than force it and get the wrong answer.

COMMON FEARS

What follows is an analysis of the common fears poker players face. For any fears not mentioned, use the general strategies provided previously in this chapter and in chapter 4 to analyze and resolve that fear.

Fear of Failure

"[The formula] for. . .success? It's quite simple, really: Double your rate of failure. You're thinking of failure as the enemy of success. But it isn't at all . . ." — Thomas J. Watson, first president of IBM.

Failure means different things to each player. For some players, failure simply means failing to reach a goal; for others, failure defines them. The fear of failure is not necessarily a bad thing. It forces some players to work hard and to do everything they can to succeed. However, for other players, it can be too disastrous to their game.

The nature of competition requires that someone has to fail, and fearing that it might be you is the most common fear in poker. The pressure to succeed makes solid players overthink decisions, only play when they feel perfect, and obsess over previously lost hands. This only makes failing more likely.

Common advice about the fear of failure, both within poker and outside of it, makes the solution seem simpler than it is for most players. The fear of failure is often caused by underlying flaws that are not well known. Resolution can only happen when *all* the flaws causing this fear are fixed.

Here's a list of the typical underlying flaws that cause the fear of failure (players typically have more than one):

- **High expectations.** Players often have ideas in their mind about how much they should be winning, how big their win rate should be, or what stakes they should be playing. These ideas are far-reaching goals and they're often the basis for high expectations. When these high expectations are not met, players are unable to understand why they failed. This results in fear and anxiety. The solution to this problem is to turn expectations into goals. Since a goal is something that a player strives for, they know there are necessary steps that need to be taken and work that needs to be done in order to reach it. An expectation is merely supposed to happen, so little to no work is done. Therefore, when expectations are regularly not met, the player begins to fear failure, but takes little to no action to discover or fix the cause of their failure. On the other hand, when a goal is not met, the player takes what was learned in their previous attempt, adjusts their strategy, and continues the work to achieve it. Players with high expectations fear failure because they haven't learned how to use failure to help them succeed.

- **Choking in big spots.** If you choke in big spots but don't know why, fear can develop. Not knowing why you choked leaves you unable to prevent it, and unable to predict when it will happen next. That uncertainty makes you protective against failing, which further paralyzes your mind and means you're more likely to choke again. Choking over a big decision happens when accumulated fear rapidly overwhelms the brain and shuts off all ability to think. *To stop choking and to reduce your accumulated fear, identify the underlying cause of your fear and follow the steps on page 66.*

- **Trying to control what you can't.** When you take poker more seriously, there's more on the line: time, money, and freedom, for example. When there's more at stake, the consequences for failing are greater, so you try to do everything you can to win. When that includes trying to control aspects of the game that can't be controlled, you set yourself up for failure. Spending time and energy trying to control variance or other players (even if subtly) means you're less focused on making sure that you're playing well. Be certain you are focused on controlling what can actually be controlled and on better understanding the factors that you can't. *For more see page 211.*

- **Failing to see success.** When smaller goals that you've accomplished in the past go unrecognized, it appears that you are failing at a higher rate. You're not; your perspective is one-sided because you've failed to recognize previous success. To correct this problem, search your poker history for the goals you've have set—small and large—and recognize the ones you have achieved. Do this steadily over a couple of weeks, as it's unlikely that you'll remember them all at once. Just writing down these accomplishments is sometimes enough to begin resolving your fears. *This cause of fear is similar to the concepts presented on page 98 regarding injustice tilt.*

- **Trying to win every session.** Often, cash game players believe that it's possible to win every session. In their mind, losing one session means they failed. Wishing it were possible to win every session sets an expectation that is beyond reach—so everything short of it becomes failure. To solve this cause of fear, prove to yourself why this wish is unattainable and why you don't want this wish to come true, and set realistic goals rather than unreasonable expectations.

- **Thinking success should be easy.** When success comes easily for a long time, players often struggle the first time they experience a big setback, such as a terrible bad run. Over time, they've come to expect success and a setback destroys that expectation. Having never faced such a challenge, they lack the skill to handle a normal setback and fear develops as they wonder if they'll ever succeed again. With the competition in poker getting strong, setbacks are going to happen. Learning how to get back to work during and after a setback is a skill. If you lack it, develop it. Success now requires hard work, especially when faced with adversity.

- **Thinking you're a failure.** If failing in poker makes you feel like a failure, there's a lot more on the line than just money. Often, players show this type of fear by not trying hard, not putting the hours in, or not working enough on their game. If they did and still failed, it would be too much for their confidence to handle. An underlying confidence problem is the cause of this fear. Once confidence is restored, their fears disappear. Refer to chapter 8.

WITHOUT SOME FAILURE, YOU CAN'T LEARN WHAT'S NEEDED TO ACHIEVE GREATER SUCCESS.

REAL FAILURE ONLY HAPPENS WHEN YOU GIVE UP.

The fear of failure is a complex problem, especially because there's potential for you to fail when trying to get rid of it. Be sure to stay aggressive in correcting the underlying cause(s) of your fear of failing—even the fear of failing to correct your fear. Expect setbacks to happen; they're a normal part of the learning process. Setbacks are not failure. Take them in stride and keep working. Lastly, since the fear of failure can be connected to motivation, tilt, and confidence, consider reviewing those chapters as well.

Fear of Success

Although less common than the fear of failure, the fear of success can be equally as detrimental. It's often difficult for players to identify because it sounds odd to fear the very thing they are trying to achieve. So why would someone fear success?

- Handling the attention that comes with success can be very tough, especially for players who aren't naturally outgoing and social.
- The spotlight can make players become arrogant, egotistical, and full of themselves. They fear becoming this way.
- They fear other players saying that they don't deserve their success and are really just a fraud who ran good.
- They undervalue their own ability and feel undeserving of their success.

Underlying the fear of success is a confidence issue. Players with stable confidence are able to succeed without having success completely change them or their approach to poker. Chapter 8 offers advice on how to develop stable confidence.

Also, be sure to have clear recognition of your pattern of fear. Then, when signs of fear show up, such as playing poorly, lacking focus, or not playing at all, you're ready to inject logic and break through your fear.

Fear of Mistakes

The fear of mistakes is caused by errors in how you view the learning process. Mistakes are an important part of this process, so fearing mistakes
suggests that you also fear learning. The fear of mistakes is subtle, so the
signs can be harder to spot. Here are a few things to keep an eye out for:

- Rushing a tough decision to get the hand over quickly and
  end the agony of uncertainty.

- Quitting after the first mistake, or perceived mistake, no matter
  how big or small.

- Treating all mistakes equally—anything less than perfection is
  not acceptable.

- Hesitating, overthinking, and second-guessing many of
  your decisions.

There are a few main reasons to fear mistakes. First, when you study and
work a lot on your game, it can lead you to believe that you won't make a
mistake twice—especially an obvious one. Consequently, when you make
a mistake twice, it's shocking; you weren't expecting it. When the disbelief wears off, it's soon replaced by questions that swirl around in your
mind about the state of your game: "How can this happen?"; "How can
I be so stupid?"; "What more can I possibly do!?" You do more work to
try and play better, but you still make the same mistake. Your game feels
out of your control and fear multiplies.

You also fear mistakes when you believe mistakes should never happen. This belief increases the pressure to play perfectly, creates performance anxiety, and ultimately leads to more mistakes. You try preventing mistakes by learning everything you can and working as hard as
possible. However, this excess of knowledge makes it harder to decide
which bit of strategy to use when under even slight pressure, and ultimately leads to mistakes.

The underlying flaws that create the fear of mistakes also create mistake tilt
(some players get angry, while others develop fear). *See pages 119-126*

to learn more about these underlying flaws. The fear of mistakes is also connected with the fear of failure, so you may find your answer there as well.

 MISTAKES ARE OPPORTUNITIES TO IMPROVE. FOCUS ON PLAYING WELL NOW, AND LEARN FROM THEM LATER.

Fear of a Bad Run

Fearing a bad run most often happens to players who've experienced many bad runs. However, with so much talk about bad runs, new players can develop the fear before even having one. Bad runs can severely hurt your bankroll, decrease your confidence, and stifle your motivation, as well as cause tilt. Each time you have a bad run, all that negative emotion piles up and stays with you. You don't forget what it's like to experience it. When you finally get on a good run, you can't even enjoy it because you know it's just a matter of time before the cards inevitably turn against you.

While a bad run does cause your bankroll to take a hit, the main reason players develop this type of fear has to do more with the experience of running bad. Sure, it sucks to lose money, but you know it's a long-term game. The tough part is being able to get through it mentally.

Running bad can drive you crazy. It's reasonable to fear all of the negative feelings that come with it. Experience the craziness of running bad enough times, and you can develop beaten dog-syndrome. Each time you run bad, you become more timid because of the thrashing that variance inflicts on you. The long-term solution here is to address the specific issues—tilt, confidence, motivation, or other fears—that make handling a bad run so difficult. Only when a bad run becomes less chaotic does the fear of having one get resolved.

After making improvements in those areas, by injecting logic you can then begin pushing through the fear as it shows up. The next time you run bad, look at it as a challenge to prove just how much better you can handle it. This approach often goes a long way in taking the fear out of something all poker players go through. Only when you know a bad run isn't going to feel like a beating does it make sense to break through the fear of a bad run. *If you haven't made improvements to how you handle running bad, <u>do not</u> take this step yet.*

CLIENT'S STORY

Pascal "Stake Monster" Tremblay
$10/$20 Heads Up NL

CARDRUNNERS COACH

"I contacted Jared when I was having some of my best months ever in terms of results, but I still had a lot of anxiety and stress related to my game that I wanted to get rid of. I played professionally full-time and the stress level—even when I was winning—was a big issue and in the long run was hurting me a lot. I was stressed before I played, while I played and even afterwards. It was a constant pressure that was just there all day.

What I came to learn was that I was consistently dreading negative variance, especially when it would last for weeks. I was constantly anxious because I never knew when I was going to lose. The possibility for a really bad day or week was always there. Whether I was winning or losing, I knew this stress was costing me. If I lost a bunch of money one day, the next day I would be scared it would happen again. If I was up a good amount, I would quit too early because I wanted to book a win, prevent a downswing, and gain some confidence. It cost me money not only when I was losing, because I would quickly fall into my C-game, but also when I was winning, because I was too focused on short-term results. I wasn't thinking about how well I was playing; I was just thinking about the immediate financial benefits or drawbacks.

It took a while to grasp some of the things Jared was telling me because the issues I was having were so deeply rooted. Things didn't instantly change overnight. It was a gradual improvement with many light-bulb moments in between sessions. His approach worked really well for me because he didn't just put a patch on the problem or tell me a quick fix.

Instead, he changed the way I think about things, not just poker, but life in general. It wasn't just what he was saying, but also the fact that I was doing work outside of our sessions, which is something I didn't even think of doing before. I had spent a lot of time reviewing hand histories and training videos, but never spent any time on myself. I never thought about it like that. It's an aspect of a poker player's game that is very often ignored and never really focused on. How can that be when our emotional state plays such a big factor at the tables?

A big thing he had me do is write, so I started a blog, and surprisingly it really helped a lot. I used it to voice my emotions towards the game and it got me understanding them better. 'If you don't understand them, you won't be able to fix them,' he would tell me. The more we talked, the more I understood, and the more I realized that I wasn't destined to feel this way. So rather than just getting pissed and thinking 'that's just the way I am,' I started thinking more about the emotional state I was in and how to change it.

Ultimately, Jared helped me identify what was really creating this fear. When I was 18, I had a really bad bout of depression. It was something I never thought would have anything to do with how I feel now 10 years later, especially in poker. Jared helped me get to the core of that, and realize that the reason I was worried about downswings was partly because I didn't want to go back to feeling like I did when I was depressed. I didn't know that at all, obviously. I thought I had fixed my depression, since I hadn't felt that way in 10 years. He helped me realize that I had just put a patch on it, and that the underlying cause wasn't resolved.

Now, I'm more constructive and positive in general, and I don't get the sense that I need to be completely fixed. Those emotions are still there; Jared didn't make them disappear like some magician, but he made the bottom of my range a lot stronger than before. I still get upset about downswings or losing several big pots in a row, but I deal with them a lot better. They are less intense, more controlled, and my C-game is a lot better, even during a downswing. I think those emotions will always be there, but I'm confident I can handle them much better now."

 "STRIVING FOR PERMANENT PERFECTION IS AN EXERCISE IN CONSTANT FRUSTRATION AND DISAPPOINTMENT."

Fear of Moving Up in Stakes

Breaking through to a new limit is easier when avoiding a common results-oriented view of moving up. Players with a fear of moving up rarely say that their goal is to establish themselves at the next limit. Instead, they just want to get to that limit and view the process as "do-or-die." They want the end result, but since a crushing defeat is a possible outcome, there's a ton of pressure riding on every decision.

To take some of the pressure off, they'll only play when the games are most profitable. A good idea, but one that feeds into the belief that moving up is all about bankroll rather than the skill needed to be successful over the long term at that limit.

The fear of moving up can often be eliminated by using a strategy that focuses more on developing skill. Rather than taking shots and hoping that you win, look at the first few times you play higher as a reconnaissance mission to gather intelligence on:

1. The strengths and weaknesses of the players.
2. The weaknesses in your game that are not exposed at your current limit—both in your poker and mental game.

After gathering this information, you can work on the weaknesses you find at your current limit without pressure or severe consequences. Then, move back and forth between limits as a way to test or work on your game. The goal is that each time you bounce back up to the higher limit, your game will be stronger. Eventually, it'll be strong enough for you to stay, and then you can begin working on establishing yourself as a solid regular. Since the fear of moving up in stakes is also closely associated with the fear of failure, review that section. Lastly, it's a good idea to decide how much of your bankroll to invest in this strategy, so you limit losses while gathering data.

Risk Aversion

In a game of variance and risk, it's not surprising that risk aversion is a common fear. Essentially, by choosing not to play in bigger games, bluffing or shoving in profitable spots, or challenging yourself against tough regulars, you are protecting your game from risk. Why? What are you concerned about? A bad run? Losing money? Losing confidence?

In being risk averse, players often unknowingly protect their game from bigger issues such as low confidence, tilt, or other fears. It's risky for them to make high-variance plays or play in bigger games because losing would trigger these mental game problems. When those bigger issues begin resolving, risk aversion also starts going away. In order to completely resolve risk aversion, it's important to push yourself to take more profitable risks at the table. At first, that might take a leap of faith, so consider setting a specific amount of money to invest in pushing yourself to take more risks. Often just knowing that your potential losses are limited helps to free you from the aversion to risk.

CLIENT'S STORY

Barry Carter
MidStakes SNGs & Cash Games
POKER JOURNALIST

"I had a crippling risk aversion that developed after a really bad down-swing. It was destroying my game. Whenever I had top pair I would fear two pair; whenever I had a set, I feared an over set; whenever I flopped the nuts, I feared I would get outdrawn. It was making me either play passively with monsters, or overbet them to avoid a cooler. 'They always have it,' I would continually say to myself.

Even though, session after session, it was the single most damaging issue I had, it was also the easiest to solve. I actually think just doing Jared's questionnaire (see page 237) cured 90% of it. Risk aversion was something I had kept in my head, so to finally let it all out on paper as I answered his questions improved the issue by leaps and bounds.

Jared helped things along by pointing out to me that I was taking an even bigger risk by doing nothing. By playing my hands passively, I was losing a ton of value. I also realized that by not playing more aggressively, I never got my opponents to fold and was always rely-ing on showdown value—I was actually encouraging my opponents to outdraw me.

I can't say that just doing the questionnaire has made me the player I am today, because I am fortunate enough to have worked intensely with Jared on all my mental game issues. The one thing I will say is if you have played with me in the last 18 months, you would never think I had a risk aversion issue; if anything you would probably think I needed to work on taking my foot off the gas a little."

7

MOTIVATION

CHANCES ARE YOU'VE COME to this chapter looking for a way to not be lazy. In the past, you've tried listening to music, watching iconic sports moments and dramatic movie clips, reading books and quotes, and making big prop bets—all in the hopes of getting motivated to play. It's as if laziness is some sort of prison, and with the right spark of inspiration you can slip past the guard and escape forever. But no matter how hard you try, laziness always catches up with you.

While you may have tried all manner of elaborate schemes to fool yourself into being motivated, have you ever confronted why you lack motivation in the first place? It's actually a simpler problem to solve than you realize.

For starters, some of you think you have a motivational problem, when in fact you have another mental game issue. If you constantly quit before going on tilt, perform poorly under pressure, or have no confidence in your game, your lack of motivation is a symptom of those problems. Often, your lack of motivation has been a problem for so long, it's easy to forget that tilt or fear was the original cause. By fixing the other mental game issues affecting motivation, most, if not all of it, will return.

Many players don't have tilt, fear, or confidence problems, and instead, are skilled procrastinators, lazy, and barely able to play when running bad. Players often don't think these problems can be eliminated, but they can be—especially laziness. Laziness is not a permanent part of your personality unless you want it to be; some players are actually quite proud of how lazy they are. Aside from being lazy, here are other motivational problems addressed in this chapter:

- You play too much or too little when running good or bad.
- You procrastinate studying or working on your game.
- You play too much and get burned out.
- You don't feel like playing after a setback, such as a big loss against a tough opponent.
- Your dreams of playing Rail Heaven make you not want to grind lower stakes.
- You improve too quickly and your game falls apart once you lose momentum.

The Nature of Motivation

It's obvious when you have motivation and when you lack it, but have you stopped to think about what motivation actually is? The answer is important, because it helps to define the underlying causes of problems with motivation.

Motivation is the emotion or energy behind achieving your goals. It's the fuel used to accomplish them. If you're lacking motivation, you either have problems with your goals or the energy you need to achieve them. Rarely do poker players say they have problems with their goals, yet every player with motivational problems has them. Here are a few examples of goal problems that will be explained in more detail later in the chapter:

- You're only after results, and have no process-oriented goals.
- You have high expectations.

- You have no short-term goals, only far-off ones.
- You reach your goals and fail to set new ones.
- You have too many goals.
- You have many interests and can't choose what you want.
- You have underlying goals such as looking good, avoiding mistakes, or keeping up your win rate.

Each of the specific motivational issues described in this chapter include some problem with goals. These problems actually decrease the amount of energy, focus, or emotion behind your goals. In other words, these flaws are leaks that drain your motivation from the poker goals you really want to achieve. It's this lack of energy that forces you to use prop bets and movie quotes to fire you up. However, there are many other sources of motivation, such as:

- Winning.
- Financial needs, such as family, paying for school, or living expenses.
- Learning and improving as a player.
- Proving people wrong.
- Feeling challenged by the game, another player, or the pursuit.
- Love for poker.
- Dreams for the future.

As you will see in this chapter, some sources of motivation are more stable and beneficial than others.

Inspiration

Although many consider them to be one and the same, there's a significant difference between motivation and inspiration. Motivation is like a marathon runner and inspiration is like a sprinter. Motivation and inspiration each play an essential part in achieving goals. Motivation is the more solid and stable energy that keeps you consistently working over the long term, while inspiration provides short, intense bursts of energy needed to get you fired up or to stay on track.

There are many ups and downs when striving to achieve goals. Inspiration is the extra juice that pushes you through tougher times and helps you reach higher levels of play. Players are inspired in many different ways and by different things—some too spontaneous to conceptualize or predict. It may be a book, movie, song, seeing another player's success, or a reward that gets your blood pumping. Successfully finding ways to inspire you can sometimes be the difference between success and failure.

While inspiration is invaluable, it can be used incorrectly. Here are two problems to look out for:

1. If you're constantly looking for new things to keep you inspired, you're relying on inspiration too much and likely compensating for underlying problems in your motivation. In other words, by playing clips of the movie *Rocky* or challenging yourself to play 100,000 hands a month, you might actually be protecting a problem that inspiration cannot fix.

2. You think a surge of inspiration makes problems such as tilt, anxiety, and a lack of confidence disappear. This is one reason why New Year's resolutions fail. People forget that it takes a long time to eliminate old habits or resolve underlying flaws. Being on an inspirational high can make these problems seem like a thing of the past.

Ultimately, when you use inspiration and motivation more efficiently, you're in a stronger position to achieve your goals.

BARRY'S TAKE

Prop Bets

Poker players often resort to making prop bets to spark their motivation. Browse any poker forum, and you are likely to see a bunch of threads where players are proposing prop bets that they can lose a certain amount of weight, play a certain number of hands, make SuperNova Elite, top a tournament leader-board, or make a certain amount of profit.

The nature of these prop bets is essentially players trying to use money as a source of inspiration to do something they want to be able to do normally, but don't have the motivation to see through. You might want to make SuperNova Elite, but you don't think you can do it unless you have money dangling in front of you.

Of course, there are many prop bets with the opposite intention in mind, where you are gambling on a perceived edge. If you are already a sick grinder, then a number of hands bet might be a very profitable proposition for you. But if you are using a prop bet to motivate you to do something you're not motivated to do, you are actually wagering a lot of money while being a big underdog. It's terrible game selection, and you are a prop bet fish.

There seems to be a distinct shift between the more old-school gamblers—who would only bet on propositions they thought were sure things—and the online generation, who want to bet on outcomes they wish would happen. You only need to hear about Amarillo Slim's legendary exploits to know he only gambled on prospects where the sucker had no chance. In these motivational bets you are the sucker, though it doesn't stop you from putting your money on the line.

In the long term, no amount of money is going to resolve the underlying issues that are causing your motivational problem(s). Only by resolving these prob-lems can you get the motivation you so desperately crave.

Stable Motivation

Finding the right mix of goals and sources of energy that drive you is key to attaining the motivational sweet spot: "stable motivation." The sweet spot is a middle ground where you are driven by the right amount of energy. This allows you to efficiently work toward your goals, maintain a steady learning curve, and perform at a high level without experiencing major ups and downs, or just downs. Stable motivation is different for each person, since we're all unique. The easiest way to find this motivational middle ground is by resolving the underlying causes of your motivational problems, which may include other mental game issues. After you do that, what remains is stable motivation to achieve your goals.

COMMON MOTIVATIONAL PROBLEMS

Laziness

Saying you're lazy is an easy way of excusing yourself from having to do something. "I would have done X, but didn't feel like it. What can I say? I'm lazy." It's as if being lazy is an incurable disease, or a character trait encoded in your DNA. If you believe deep down that laziness is permanent, it would be illogical for you to try anything to change it. However, laziness is not a permanent trait. It takes some work to break out of it, but this section can make that task easier.

Laziness is a skill, that for better or worse, has been learned. You have learned the skill of doing something else. You have learned how to grind a large volume of television or sleep, rather than learning how to knuckle down and play longer sessions and work on your game. Instead of learning how to be productive, you've learned how to be lazy—and you're quite good at it.

It's impossible to have no motivation. Think of being lazy as having a strong motivation to sleep for hours, watch TV, or mindlessly surf the internet. While that might seem like just a changing around of words, stating it that way is important in understanding and fixing the problem.

Laziness can happen for many reasons. It may have developed early in your life if you weren't pushed to excel. Or maybe it developed after college when completely on your own, or after making good money because you no longer felt you had to make more. Here's an example to help explain how laziness can develop and how to solve it:

Often people become lazy when the structure they are used to having in their lives is gone. When living with parents, going to school, or working for someone else, you don't have to think much about what to do, you just have to do it. The value of having that structure provided for you often goes unrecognized until you're completely out on your own. Now you have to do both—decide what to do and do it. That extra layer may not seem like much, but it makes life, or poker, a lot harder and often leads to laziness.

When beginning to work on your laziness or any other motivational problem, try approaching poker like you're running a small business. You're in charge of when and where to play, how much to play, what stakes and games to play in, when and what to study, and who to get help from. It's your responsibility to analyze your poker and mental games, stay up-to-date with the latest software and strategy, and more.

There's a lot to decide and to do. If you're lacking the skills to successfully run your business, you appear lazy. Here are a few simple ways to improve these skills:

1. Identify all the good things that you're doing, no matter how insignificant they seem.
2. Write out a list of what you need to be doing.
3. Prioritize the most important things you need to be doing.
4. Make a reasonable plan for how to start doing them.
5. Write down the excuses you previously made to avoid doing them.

6. Write down why each excuse is flawed or false.
7. Commit to executing your plan and avoiding excuses.

Realizing there's something you can do about laziness means you at least have a chance of permanently staying out of the prison that laziness puts you in.

DOING WHAT IS LESS FUN NOW, MEANS YOU CAN HAVE MUCH MORE FUN IN THE FUTURE.

WORK HARDER WHEN IT'S HARD, AND EVENTUALLY IT'LL BECOME EASY FOR REAL.

THINK OF ONE THING YOU CAN DO TO BE PRODUCTIVE. BUILDING MOMENTUM HAS TO START SOMEWHERE.

Procrastination

Constantly delaying and putting off what's important defines the skill of procrastinating. There's a lot you can be doing, such as reviewing hands, watching training videos, reading books, analyzing your game, posting on and reading forums, working with a coach, etc. It's easy to put work off when it seems like, "there's always tomorrow."

Of course, for procrastinators, tomorrow is a leprechaun—a mystical entity that isn't real. When tomorrow becomes today, your work once again gets delayed until tomorrow. The longer it goes on, the more likely you are to delay working; especially since each day keeps adding more and more videos, hands, and forum posts to review.

Tomorrow never comes in the way that you imagine. Only when you're under intense pressure from running bad, your win rate/profit drops, or you're preparing for a big tournament will you start cramming in all of the work that you've been avoiding. Unfortunately, without extreme intensity, working at a normal pace feels boring and like a major grind. So, you end up depending on an intense pressure to learn, which often leads to burnout and perpetuates your pattern of procrastination.

Other problems that result from working too intensely on your game include:

- Experiencing continual ups and downs in how well you're playing.
- Getting overtaken by players who work more consistently.
- Having a false impression of how much you can actually learn. It's impossible to learn skills to the level of Unconscious Competence that quickly.
- Feeling more confused because you now have much more to think about when playing.

If you want to stop procrastinating, you first must eliminate the belief, "there's always tomorrow." Today is when improvement happens, not just in your game but also in reducing procrastination. Today is your only opportunity to improve. Tomorrow is a fantasy.

That doesn't mean you have to do it *all* today; developing consistency also means working at a steadier pace. Besides, when learning poker skills or knowledge to the level of Unconscious Competence, working for 15 minutes per day (rather than by cramming in three hours every other week) is the most efficient method. That is not true for everyone, of course, and it doesn't mean that you're restricted to working for 15 minutes at a time. However, if you're currently doing no work, then 15 minutes a day is a good start.

TODAY IS THE DAY TO IMPROVE. TOMORROW IS A FANTASY. IF YOU WAIT UNTIL TOMORROW, YOU'LL HAVE TWICE THE AMOUNT OF WORK TO DO.

Running Good and Bad

Variance does not cause motivational problems; it unearths them. Running good or bad provides an excellent way to identify the specific motivational or other mental game problems affecting your game. Thanks to variance, problems that may normally be small leaks accumulate into bigger problems. The pressure that variance puts on your game brings them to light, and tells you what to be working on.

When you are running bad, you might lack motivation because:

- You feel destined to lose = **Injustice Tilt**
- Working on your game seems like a waste of time = **Hopelessness**
- You question your ability = **Low Confidence**
- You drop down in limits and have trouble playing enough hands = **Low Confidence or Fear of Failure**
- You don't want to go on tilt = **Any type of tilt**

A period of good variance can have a similar effect on your motivation because:

- You've won enough and don't need to play anymore = **Goal Problems**
- It feels too easy, as if you're printing money = **Overconfidence**
- You want to book a win = **Risk Aversion or Hate-losing Tilt**
- You feel so good about your game, you don't need to work on it = **Overconfidence**

- You don't want to lose money back, or have the feeling that losing brings = **Fear of Failure**

The above are a handful of the problems running good or bad can expose.
It's important to consistently be working to improve them, even when you're
running normally and they're not being exposed by variance. The only way
to know if these issues are gone or how much progress you've made is by
analyzing your mental game the next time you run well or run terribly. That's
your test, so be prepared and consistently work on them until you pass.

Burnout

Burnout is a unique motivational issue because it's actually caused by intense
motivation. Even though players who regularly suffer from burnout often think
they are lazy, the opposite is true. They are so motivated after playing and
working themselves into the ground that when their mind is extremely fatigued
and needs rest, they criticize themselves for not wanting to play, being easily
distracted, being bored, or feeling tired. They're not lazy—they need rest!

Here are two things to keep in mind about burnout:

1. It's possible to mistake burnout for another motivational problem, since the symptoms are similar.

2. Burnout also makes you more susceptible to other mental game
problems such as tilt.

UNDERESTIMATING STRESS

Generally, players significantly underestimate the amount of stress and
pressure they are under when playing poker. Career, family, achievement,
and respect all add more pressure to every decision, and thus require the
player to have more energy to consistently play at a high level. Players who
underestimate the stress in poker are often the ones who are most critical
of themselves. They often end up thinking that they're being lazy, when in
reality constant high levels of stress have caused them to burn out.

Burnout isn't an excuse; it's a real cause of motivational problems.

Highly motivated people burn out when they go through a long period of intense motivation without getting proper rest. The concept of burnout in mental terms is roughly the same as it is with physical training. When runners train too hard, their performance suffers because overworked muscles become fatigued. Similarly, when poker players play too much and for too long, their performance suffers because their mental muscle is exhausted.

Here are a few ideas on how to break this cycle:

- During times when you're intensely motivated, ease off the throttle just a bit. When emotion–even motivation–is too high, it can cause you to play sub-optimally and slow down the learning process.

- Recognize the early signs of your pattern of burnout, and take steps to get proper rest, such as sleep and exercise, to prevent the problem from getting worse.

- Take at least one day off per week and five days off per month. On your days off, think about and do other things than poker.

- Have a hobby other than poker that you enjoy doing and don't take too seriously.

- For online players, make sure to take some time away from all electronics each day.

- Evaluate your game at the end of each day that you play. This helps you mentally put poker down and allows your brain to relax.

Goal Problems

Goals are essential to motivation because they define its direction. This topic often covers entire chapters in other books; but to keep things simple, here are descriptions of the most common goal problems listed earlier in this chapter:

Results-oriented goals only. When results are poor and they are the only way you define your skill or progress in the game, losing motivation makes sense. Since you're guaranteed to go through periods of poor results, it's important to learn how to maintain motivation throughout these periods. To do that, add process-oriented goals such as improving tilt control, reducing the number of mistakes, improving decision making, or increasing quality hours played. Then, when results are poor, if you're also making progress in other areas, you'll remain motivated. You're not eliminating results goals. Money, winning, SuperNova Elite, and other results goals matter. You're diversifying your goals in poker, just like you diversify an investment portfolio. Adding process-oriented goals is especially important in poker because you have control of your ability to achieve these goals in the short run.

High expectations. Often players have expectations that are so high, they're nearly impossible to achieve. For example, it's common for players to expect to easily play 40 hours more per month than usual, win a large amount of money, or move up in stakes quickly. These goals seem easy in their mind, but they're ignoring reasons why in reality they'll be tough to achieve. When they often fall short of reaching these high expectations, players get stuck in the disappointment of failure and they lose motivation. They're dejected about failing, even though they were wrong to believe they could achieve such things in the first place. Really, they ought to be setting goals. When they have goals, they strive to figure out how to achieve them. Then, when they fall short of a goal, they readjust their strategy and keep moving forward. Unless you have solid proof of what you can expect to accomplish, turn every expectation into a goal, and then figure out how to achieve it.

Far-away goals. When you have a big dream or long-term goal without any smaller targets, it can be easy to lose motivation when things go poorly. These setbacks, such as a downswing, can make you feel as if your dream or goal is farther away, and can cause you to lose hope. Instead, break your long-term goal into more manageable chunks. This way it's easier to recover from a setback and continue moving forward. Having smaller or short-term goals is important so you can see progress along the way. These small victories are essential in keeping you motivated for the long haul.

Reach a milestone, now what? If you win a tournament, have your biggest month ever, move up in stakes, go pro, or make SuperNova or SuperNova Elite without setting your next goal, you can be lacking motivation simply because you no longer have something to play for.

Indecision. There are a lot of possible goals to strive for, both within poker and outside of it. When you don't know what you want, you end up doing a lot of random things that make it seem as if you're unmotivated. Really, you're undecided. Rather than getting down that you aren't accomplishing anything, see this period for what it is: an exploration. When there are a lot of options, you're essentially standing at the base of several mountains trying to decide which one to climb. You're in the process of gathering information, eventually needing to make a decision about what you want. To make the process go faster, regularly write down your options, evaluate them, and get feedback from other players.

Underlying goals. Sometimes players are motivated to avoid embarrassment, mistakes, criticism, losing money, or having their win rate drop. It's rare for players to think of these as goals, but when viewed that way, their behavior—such as avoiding playing—makes a lot more sense. These underlying goals are a problem because you spend energy on them, rather than on the goals in poker that you really want to achieve. After identifying these underlying goals in your game, resolve the reason you want to achieve them, and you'll have more motivation for the goals that are really important.

Personal goals. If you need to play poker, but aren't motivated by anything within poker, consider how poker fits into your life. Then set personal goals that poker can help you to accomplish. The motivation to get hands in comes back when poker has greater importance in your life.

CLIENT'S STORY

Matt "mbolt1" Bolt
$3/$6 to $50/$100 NLHE

DRAGTHEBAR COACH

"Working with Jared really helped me get to SuperNova Elite in 2010. It was never a question of whether I would do it. It was a question of how well I could play having to grind a ton of hands while I was running bad. PokerStars doesn't care if I win or lose; I don't get any more VPPs for playing well. Obviously, I wanted to win money in the process, but results-based goals are terrible; goals like winning a certain amount of money are stupid. I just had to play well.

Motivation was definitely an issue early on, but became way less of one as I got used to the idea of grinding no matter what cards came out. There were several 100k hand stretches where I played my best and didn't win. I can look back at it, and say with confidence that I couldn't have played much better. Goals around making money just lead to bad thoughts about being able to control variance, when obviously I can't. Jared helped me realize that I needed to focus on what I controlled, which is how well and how much I played. Having those goals for me was essential for getting SuperNova Elite."

Freerolling Your Talent

There are a lot of smart, young people in poker these days. People who breezed through school and even college have quickly climbed the ranks at the tables. They're the equivalent of talented, successful athletes who never faced any major challenges as they moved through the ranks. Facing adversity for the first time is shocking and they don't know what to do. Success came so easily that they weren't forced to acquire the work ethic, discipline, organization, and sheer will needed to get through tough times.

Being able to handle adversity is a skill shared by highly successful people in any competitive industry or sport. Talent alone is no longer enough. For example, when scouting future NFL quarterbacks, coaches are wary about drafting players who haven't experienced some kind of adversity on or off the field. Coaches want to know that they'll be able to handle the challenges they'll inevitably face in the NFL.

If you're struggling to find motivation when facing adversity in poker for the first time, whether it's a terrible run or tougher games, now is the time to become mentally stronger. Here's how to avoid falling into the trap of relying only on your talent:

1. Reaffirm or adjust your goals.
2. Clearly define why you want to achieve them.
3. Make a realistic plan for how to achieve them.
4. Prioritize your time to fit in the necessary work.
5. Get help from people with a strong work or study ethic.
6. Write down the top five things that are likely to throw you off or make it hard to work.
7. Avoid the missteps from step 6 by injecting logic and using something inspirational.

Facing adversity is a challenge. However, the reward is out there for those who can face adversity head-on and come out stronger on the other side.

Stop Dreaming

It's good to have dreams. Many great accomplishments began with a person or player dreaming of what they wanted. Unfortunately, some players get so caught up in their dreams that they take on a life of their own. When they imagine what winning a bracelet or a huge sum of money would be like, real emotion is felt and it's so strong that in a strange sort of way, the dream already feels real.

When you believe your dreams are already real, it feels like they are destroyed at the first sign of trouble. You don't envision adversity when dreaming or fantasizing. In your mind, your dreams come true easily; nothing is going to stop you. That is, until you hit the inevitable bumps in the road. Consequently, you're completely unprepared to handle the real struggles that stand between you and your dreams, and you lose motivation.

The solution is to turn your dreams into goals. Take the dream and make a plan for *how* to make it real. Identify what it is going to take, the skills needed to get there, and perhaps just as importantly, what to do when adversity knocks you down.

WHAT'S ONE THING YOU CAN DO RIGHT NOW TO MAKE THIS DREAM A REALITY?

Absence of Learning

You're bored. Poker has become a tough grind. Autopiloting is too tough to fight, so you end up playing poorly. After several days this way, your desire to play steadily decreases until you find it hard to motivate yourself to play. There are many reasons for this scenario; one reason many players don't account for is the absence of learning.

Learning is exciting and it keeps your mind active, focused, and engaged. When there is nothing to learn in poker, or when you believe you have learned something to the level of Unconscious Competence, it's illogical for your mind to focus. So you get bored. This process is called "habituation," and it's one way the brain is energy efficient.

Thankfully, there is plenty you can do about this and these methods can help:

- **Use boredom as a cue.** When you find yourself getting bored playing poker, use it as a sign that it's time to look for something new to learn, even if it's something simple.

- **Dig deep into the smaller details of the game.** Having already learned the big stuff, the next place for you to become skilled is in the spots with smaller edges. This is the basis of mastery, and elite players do it all the time.

- **Remember that mastery is a moving target.** Often players believe there isn't anything new to learn. This is impossible. Although it may be hard to find, there is always something to learn, and the reward is there for those who work to find it.

- **Use the process model to consistently learn and to focus on small details.**

- **Get a coach or friend to have sweat sessions and discuss hands with.** Not only does this stimulate learning, it also doesn't hurt to have an impartial critique of your game.

- **Continue learning until skills reach Unconscious Competence.** Often players assume they've learned skills to the level of Unconscious Competence, when they actually haven't. Only when you play under intense pressure and consistently retain the skills you've learned can you prove ownership of them. Until then, keep learning.

- **Change games to get you thinking in a different way.**

- **Play in tougher games to discover and assess the weaknesses in your game.**

- **Take a break.** You might be burned out.

Jordan "iMsoLuckyO" Morgan
Tournament player & Mid-stakes NLHE
FULL TILT POKER RED PRO

"I reached a pretty high level of success early in my career; then I got a sponsorship deal with Full Tilt where I could make decent chunks of money just grinding out hands. I wasn't putting any work into my game, and ended up breaking even for a long time. I was pretty miserable for quite a while because I wasn't improving and I wasn't winning.

It took Jared several sessions to get through to me, but he made me realize I had kind of built a bubble around myself where I expected the success I had early in my career to continue. I had been living in a bubble for so long, thinking, 'this [breaking-even] should not be happening,' but I wasn't putting in the work like I did early in my career. I set several goals early in my career, and after the Full Tilt deal I reached them all by the time I was 23 years old. So between 23 and 25, I just treaded water and expected everything to keep coming easily. But it doesn't work like that.

It was enlightening and freeing to realize I was not as good as I thought. When poker is going well and you experience positive variance for a long time, you get to where you feel invincible—everything you are doing is right and will stay right forever. When things go poorly, you don't want to admit that it might be your fault; you just want to ignore it and move on. It took me a lot of self-realization to admit this and get back to working.

Now it feels good to see progress because I know I'm working hard for it. My goals now are much more about improving on a daily or weekly basis—realistic stepping stones. Before, when I started cash games I would say to myself, 'I want to be playing $10/$20 in a year,' but I wouldn't have a process to get there. Now, I am on a path where I can take little steps to be better every day. Jared helped me realize that it takes a lot of small steps to get on the right path to where I want to go."

"POKER IS HARDER THAN I THINK IT IS; I SHOULDN'T BEAT MYSELF UP TOO MUCH WHEN RESULTS ARE POOR."

Numb to Emotion

Conventional poker psychology often suggests that players handle negative emotion by being numb, desensitized, and robotic. This approach typically has a short-term benefit, but one long-term consequence is that it decreases the emotion that's used for motivation. Sure, you won't tilt from a bad beat, but winning doesn't feel that good either. Eventually, playing poker will feel like a constant grind because there's no emotion to fuel you.

Correcting this problem means you have to begin experiencing emotions again. It may be tough since tilt, fear, or confidence can reappear. If they do, use the information in the respective chapters to help you deal with them. Inspiration can also help to fire you up in the short term. Find some music, a motivational speech, an inspiring scene in a film, or some other source of inspiration to kick your motivation back into gear.

Hopeless

When your motivation is at its lowest point, you feel hopeless. Feeling hopeless means that you believe there is nothing you can do to achieve your goals. So you might think:

- "No matter what I do, it's not going to make a difference. Why bother?"

- "What's the point? I'm just going to fail anyway."

- "I can't see how things are going to turn around. I should just quit."

When you believe there is no way to affect the outcome, it's logical that you wouldn't feel motivated. Losing motivation to this degree is connected to an underlying confidence problem that is typically caused by believing, at a deeper level, that you have more control over an outcome than you actually do. One example of this is thinking that running bad is completely your fault. On a logical level, you know that isn't true; but at the level of Unconscious Competence you believe it, and hopelessness predictably sets in.

To become more hopeful, read chapter 8.

8

CONFIDENCE

THE VARIANCE IN POKER can turn confidence into a rollercoaster ride that rises and falls along with the cards. Win and you're riding high. Lose and you're down, and may even have to sit out the next few trips around.

Results shouldn't control your confidence, you know that, but you still can't stop from going through the highs and lows of winning and losing. While riding a heater, you try not to book wins, play too many hands, or take on tougher opponents, but they are too hard to resist. Winning feels great. As you win more, you also win more confidence. Until variance turns on you.

You are so caught up in riding the high, you don't see losing coming. Suddenly, your results take a nosedive and destroy your confidence. "It's variance, you're playing fine. Just keep at it, eventually the cards will turn around," your friends or coach might say to ease your mind. You want to believe them, and logically you know they're right, but all the money you're losing makes you feel terrible about your game.

When confidence is completely tied to results, there's no way to avoid riding the confidence rollercoaster. The best way to stop these emotional swings and develop "stable confidence" is by learning a set of rarely talked about poker skills and resolving the underlying flaws in your confidence.

The Nature of Confidence

It is common to think that you need confidence in order to have success or to win. The assumption is that if you lack confidence, you won't succeed in sports, when starting a business, or playing poker. Having confidence is important, but not as much as many players seem to think.

After a large enough sample, regardless of how you feel about your ability, your results tell the real story. Having confidence does help you to perform at a higher level than when you're lacking it; however, that still doesn't mean you have the skill to succeed. Being confident that you can win doesn't mean you will, just as lacking confidence doesn't mean you won't.

Confidence is the most complex of the four major emotions covered in this book. Confidence should accurately be a reflection of the results and skill you've proven in poker. If you have attained solid results over a large sample of hands that prove you have real skill in the game, logically you should feel confident. On the other hand, if over that sample your results are terrible, logically you should lack confidence. However, that's not always the case. There are players without a proven track record who display more confidence than other players who have a huge win rate over millions of hands. Conversely, there are players who have crushed for years who lose confidence after just one losing session.

Confidence is an unreliable measure of results and skill for two reasons:

1. Underlying flaws in your mental game create inaccurate feelings about the quality of your game.
2. Players use short-term results to form the foundation of their confidence. However, short-term results are unreliable for proving a player's skill, therefore the basis of their confidence is also unreliable.

In most other competitive arenas, results are the easiest way to prove a player's skill level. But the fact is, such a large sample is required to determine your skill that by the time you get it, your skill has changed. In the short term you can't definitively prove your skill, you can only estimate it. That's one of the challenges in poker and what makes it perhaps harder than any other form of competition.

If you can only prove your level of poker skill months—if not years—down the line, what do you do in the short term? If you're like most players, you still use short-term results to define your skill, which is a bit like getting an opinion on your game from someone who has watched you play one hand. To keep variance from causing you to go insane, you've likely tried these options:

1. Build a proven track record over years.
2. Play a high volume to reach the long term faster.
3. Ignore, block out, or desensitize yourself to results. The intent is to prevent your emotions from going through cycles of over- and under-confidence as your results fluctuate.
4. Create the illusion in your mind that you're a solid player, even if you can't prove it.

Since your level of confidence determines many of your decisions in poker, it's important to have your confidence be as stable as possible. That's why the goal of this chapter is to help you build stable confidence.

Stable Confidence

Having stable confidence means that your confidence never swings to extremes because of variance. This is possible when your game is built on a set of results and skills that give you more certainty about the strength of your game in the short term. When your confidence is stable, minor fluctuations actually help to improve your game. You won't get too down or critical of how you played. And, in equal measure, you won't delude yourself into thinking you've mastered poker.

With stable confidence, negative emotions such as tilt or fear are easily handled without feeling robotic or numb. You have the right amount of emotion to be focused, objective, calm, and levelheaded. You feel solid about your skills relative to the games you're playing. You can think clearly through all of the pieces of information in a hand, and you can make a good decision. When you make a mistake, you're objective enough to take note of it and move on.

You're often in the zone.

In a sense, you can consider stable confidence as the middle ground between overconfidence and under-confidence. That doesn't mean you feel neutral, robotic, or numb. In fact, it's quite the opposite. You are full of emotion, but that emotion is no longer tied to short-term results, and is instead tied to elements of the game that you control. As a result, you're:

- Playing at a high level
- Able to make objective decisions
- Aware of your strengths and weaknesses
- Aware of your opponents' strengths and weaknesses
- Clearheaded
- Trusting of your instincts
- Not overly emotional, but motivated and energetic
- Challenged
- Interested
- Learning from each session
- Prepared to work on your game

Each player experiences stable confidence in slightly different ways, so a good exercise is to write down a short description of your poker and mental game when your confidence is ideal. That means it's not neutral or too high, and certainly not low; so what is it? This is important because the way to create stable confidence is by removing mental game flaws and by improving the poker skill deficits that force you out of it. By clearly defining what stable confidence means to you, identifying when you're under- or overconfident is easier. Then you can take action to re-stabilize confidence in the moment.

Under-confident and Overconfident

Although under- and overconfidence seem to be complete opposites, they actually originate from the same central issues: mental game flaws and poker skill deficits. On a sick run of cards your confidence becomes super high. Conversely, a long run of losing can cause your confidence to be lower than ever. When your confidence overreacts to winning or losing, it's caused by the same flaw. Your confidence just reacts differently depending on the circumstances.

Here are common characteristics of under- and overconfidence:

Under-confident

- Depressed or down about your game.
- Feels like you're not making progress.
- Previous success means nothing.
- Play lower stakes trying to regain confidence.
- Lack of trust in your game.
- Constantly change strategy or switch games.
- Feel pessimistic and assume you'll lose.
- Self-destructive as if you want to lose.
- Feel desperate to find the answer to your poor results.
- Embarrassed about moving down in stakes or by the stakes you're playing.
- Play less poker overall.

Overconfident

- Feel like you can beat anyone.
- Poker seems easy. You assume you'll win each time you play.
- Don't play as much.
- Regularly book wins.
- Your dream of playing nosebleeds seems certain to come true.
- Feel a euphoric high.
- Flaws or leaks seem to be gone from your game.
- Berate other players and talk about how terrible they are.
- Try to win every pot and play much more aggressively.
- Play outside your bankroll.
- Dismiss advice from good players.
- Feel impatient.
- Become complacent and stop working on your game.

It's easy for most players to recognize when they lack confidence, and much harder for them to spot when they have too much. While having too much confidence is just as destructive as not having enough, it's often overlooked as a major problem. In fact, for some talented players, being overconfident was much worse because it busted them from the game. Winner's tilt, as it's often called, can cause players to ignore basic bankroll management and game selection. While riding a variance-fueled high, these players were easily convinced that their greatness meant that they could beat anyone. At the time, the strong belief they had in their game and decisions that followed seemed justified, except reality told a much different story.

When you are overconfident, the positive feelings about your game are so strong that they seem to make weaknesses, tilt, distractions, and even losing disappear from your game. Poker seems to be an ATM dishing out easy money. So, you start playing more hands and it almost doesn't matter how you play, you still continue to win. It's a variance-fueled high and you sort of know it, but the emotions make that *minor* detail not matter. You book wins and don't play as much because the game feels so easy. At times when you normally would be playing, you're instead calculating how much money you'll be making. Perhaps you even dream of what's to come: playing high stakes against the best, winning a huge tournament, turning pro, traveling the world, and buying things you've always wanted.

As the saying goes, "The higher you climb, the harder you fall." When your variance-fueled high inevitably ends, you're blindsided by losing. Confidence takes a direct hit, and when the shock wears off, you're left picking up the pieces of your shattered game.

When confidence is at a low point, there's a negative, depressed, and pessimistic feel to your game. There's often a lot of self-criticism, questioning, and poor motivation as well. You're moody, and it starts to affect your personal life. You decline invitations from your friends to go out and snap at others for no real reason. You don't work on your game—you completely change how you play, or change games altogether. Online players occasionally delete entire databases in the hopes that a fresh start will rejuvenate their confidence. Sometimes when confidence is so low, losing can actually feel good. *See page 147 for more.*

DEVELOPING STABLE CONFIDENCE

Having stable confidence might seem to be an idealized version of confidence, but developing it can actually be straightforward once you understand how to correct a unique set of mental game flaws and poker skills.

First is a set of poker skills that all poker players already have, but relative to their actual technical poker skill, can be weak enough to cause confidence problems. This skill set is similar to the foundational skills described in chapter 2, where fixing errors in your approach to learning and performance eliminated problems in your mental game. Here, you may solve all of your confidence problems by improving the following three skills:

- The skill of recognizing variance
- The skill of recognizing your skill
- The skill of recognizing your opponents' skill

Even after developing these poker skills, many players still can't create the stable confidence they need to weather variance in the short term. Achieving stable confidence can only happen when you resolve underlying flaws in your mental game that create illusions in your confidence. These illusions act like trap doors under your poker skills that spring open when triggered by circumstances at the table, most commonly when running terrible or like god.

The mind is powerful, and it can be easy to get caught up believing things about your game that are not real. While variance does a great job of feeding these illusions, a player must also believe them. A player believes these illusions when they have specific flaws at the level of Unconscious Competence. The three most common illusions are:

- Illusion of control
- Illusion of permanence
- Illusion of learning

These illusions, as well as how to develop the mental skills necessary to resolve them, are discussed in detail later in this chapter.

When you strengthen the three overlooked poker skills, and resolve the flaws creating illusions in your mind, the result is stable confidence. Since even established players go through periods of uncertainty in their game, having stable confidence doesn't mean you're always at your ideal confidence level. Instead, stable confidence means that your confidence is built on something more solid than just results. That way in the short run, no matter how you're running, the ups and downs in your confidence are minimized.

The Skill of Recognizing Variance

The most important of these three skills is the ability to recognize variance while playing. While you can't control variance, the ability to spot it makes you better able to assess your skill and the skill of your opponents. Since so many decisions are made based on your perceived edge in the game, accuracy is critical. If your skill in recognizing variance is weak, your estimate of your edge will be off.

Variance is one of the most important concepts in poker. Yet, there's only a small amount of instructional material available on how to recognize variance while playing, beyond the obvious coolers, bad beats, and suck-outs. This has resulted in a ton of skilled poker players being terrible at recognizing variance.

When was the last time you admitted to running well during a session, playing poorly, or another player playing a hand well against you? Online players constantly use all-in EV as a measure of variance, while freely admitting it only accounts for a small amount of the total.

Lacking the skill of recognizing variance while playing may not seem like a big deal. However, just imagine what would happen to your game if you had as much skill at spotting variance as you did at spotting profitable places to bluff. Automatically, you'd become better at evaluating how you played in the short run, identifying mistakes, and knowing the degree to which variance impacted your results. Not only would it be easier to play well, it would be easier to add new lines to your game.

It's very difficult to calculate the impact of variance on a hand, but as with any other skill, you get better the more you work at it. Here are a few ideas how:

1. While playing, note or mark the hands where you suspect variance was a factor.

2. Before looking at the results of a session (obviously not possible for tournaments), take a snapshot assessment of how you ran. Was it neutral? Did you run well? Did you run bad? Estimate variance by giving it a rating and, use the hands where you believe it was a factor to back up your opinion. You might instinctively look more for the spots where you ran badly, so be sure to look for good variance, too.

3. Combine your estimate of variance and your estimate of how you played (more about this in the next section), and compare it to your actual results.

4. Since there is such a void in poker instruction, talk with other players about how to analyze or estimate the impact of variance in certain spots. Then work to get better at it. On the surface, it may seem too difficult to move beyond the obvious, but you've already improved since you first started playing. Plus, even just working to better understand variance means your confidence will be more stable.

The Skill of Recognizing Your Skill

Just reading this title can make you scratch your head a bit. This skill essentially is the ability to know how you are playing in real time. Often, players rely on results to know their skill, but short-term results are unreliable. For example, it's common for players to assume that they made a mistake just because they lost the hand; or conversely assume they're playing well because they're winning. Instead, by developing more knowledge about their game, players automatically have a stronger sense of how well they're playing without needing results to tell them.

While it's impossible to know definitively how you're playing, the stronger your recognition of your skill, the more stable your confidence becomes. Here are a few ideas on how to improve your ability to recognize your poker skill:

1. Identify the strengths in your game that are proven to be at the level of Unconscious Competence. These are the skills that always show up no matter how badly you're playing. One of the ways to identify these strengths is by analyzing the solid parts of your game when on tilt or under emotional pressure for another reason. *For more, refer to chapter 2 and the section, "Using Tilt to Improve Your Play" on page 150.*

2. Create a list of the greatest weaknesses in your game. These are all of the major mistakes that show up when playing at your worst. These weaknesses can be hard to swallow because they are so basic relative to your best. However, identifying them means you know what to improve, which is better than not knowing. Plus, since these weaknesses are often connected to tilt or other mental game issues, recognizing them while you're playing helps you to spot those issues so you can take action to control them.

3. Identify the entire range of your game from your current absolute worst, to your current absolute best. To do that, think about what mistakes you make when playing your B-game, what makes your B-game better than your C-game, and what defines your A-game. Having that knowledge allows you to make better adjustments because you know how you are playing. *For more details on this analysis, see page 122.*

4. Evaluate your game regularly. After every session, analyze how you played, what improved, and what needs more work. Set goals for the next session based on your evaluation.

You can also use these steps to improve the skill of recognizing your mental game skill. Having detailed knowledge of your mental game also contributes to stable confidence and better decision making when playing. For example, if you know you have the ability to control tilt, confidence in your overall game increases.

The Skill of Recognizing Your Opponents' Skill

The final overlooked poker skill further strengthens your ability to recognize your edge in the game, and gives you a stronger sense of the accuracy of your results in the short term. Here are some ideas on how to become better at recognizing skill in your opponents:

1. Identify instances when you suspect your opponents played well and played poorly. What did they do well that you can apply to your own game, and what did they do poorly that you can exploit in the future? Resist the urge to prematurely label someone a fish. Instead, be objective and specific in assessing their strengths and weaknesses relative to your game. The stronger this skill, the more objective you become about your opponents' play, and thus your own.

2. Keep your opinion of their game open. This way, you can easily adjust when a player does something that contradicts your opinion of them. Otherwise, you might miss adjustments that they're making to your game.

3. Analyze key hands by thinking about the hand from their position.

4. Take a few small notes throughout the session on the players at your table, even if nothing glaringly positive or negative can be said about their game.

5. Ask better players for advice on how they recognize skill in their opponents.

BARRY'S TAKE

Defining Your Edge

Defining edge is such an important part of being a successful poker player—especially if you rely on the game to make a living. After all, it should be the number-one component of your game selection process.

Yet, no matter how important this concept is, there are few arenas in life other than poker where most of the participants routinely misjudge their own skill level. You only have to look at staking request threads on poker forums to see how everyone claims to be +EV against the field (that they currently don't have the money to compete with), but rarely are they able to back up their claims with a proven track record.

Everyone seems to think that they are the best player at their table, and often low-stakes players critique the abilities of elite players and make naïve claims, such as nosebleed players like Daniel Negreanu "couldn't beat $100NL." I've interviewed hundreds of successful professional players, and this trend goes all the way to the top; they all seem to think that they are one of the best, and unluckier than most.

I'm not suggesting that if you have found yourself in one of these groups that you are wrong in your assessment of your edge. However, if you were to believe what poker players say to be true, you would wonder where exactly the losing players are. It seems that everyone is a winning player, everyone they play against is bad, and they always seem to go out of the tournament to a bad beat.

It's understandable; nobody wants to face up to their own shortcomings. You never hear someone say that their expectation is to lose $11 an hour against someone. For that matter, you rarely even hear a player say that they are playing in a game where they are a dog because they want to use it as a learning experience.

Poker offers endless opportunity for delusion. Thanks to variance, you can choose to believe that you are unfortunate when you lose, and that you crushed the game when you win. That's how you can end up playing in games that you have no place being in and losing a lot of money, while all the time blaming the poker gods for your losses.

Stable confidence plays an important part in accurately evaluating your edge and your real skill level—not just your opinion or what you wish was your edge. It has to be based on something more solid, which is why working on your skills of recognizing variance, your skill, and your opponents' skill are so important. Not only is it vital to making sure you are playing in profitable games, it is also a very important way of ensuring that you are always striving to improve your game.

Illusion of Control
There are times when you believe that you have more influence on the outcome than you actually do. This could be something as harmless as shouting "one time" before a river card is dealt, or something more damaging, such as trying to win every hand. The illusion of control affects your beliefs about your game, your opponents, and variance.

Illusions about your game. Believing you are in more control of your poker or your mental game is the primary reason for instability in your confidence. Here are the three most common causes:

1. **Believing you can win every hand**. Mostly you play normally, but when tilting or running hot, this belief gets exposed and you end up trying to win every hand. *For advice on how to correct this flaw, see page 114.*

WINNING DOESN'T MEAN YOU PLAYED WELL.

2. **Malfunctioning Mind.** A player who hasn't worked to improve their tilt problem, predictably loses control when faced with a barrage of tilt-inducing things. At that time, they lose control in large part because the brain shuts off their ability to think. However, players often expect to be able to remain in control of their game regardless of how intense their emotions. This illusion of control happens when they fail to realize that the brain is the one in control. It has the power to shut down their ability to think, which prevents them from using higher brain functions necessary to remain in control.

   Now that you have some knowledge of how the brain works, focus your efforts on gaining real control of your emotions by using the strategies outlined in chapter 4.

3. **Entitlement Tilt.** Believing that you have the right to win, especially against fish, means that at the level of Unconscious Competence, your sense of control is exaggerated. It's likely that you're a solid player, but no one in poker, no matter how good they are, deserves to win all of the time. *See page 130 for how to correct this problem.*

Illusions about your opponents. When you feel a sense of dominance and power over your opponents, part of that feeling may be an illusion. While feeling confident that you can beat them is important, this illusion makes you overconfident when crushing them, and under-confident when getting crushed.

The section on revenge tilt relates entirely to this illusion. Here are the two more common causes:

1. **Owning Souls.** Thinking you own another player's soul is an illusion. It's based on the very subtle flaw that you think you can be in control of another player. This sense of power creates good feelings, or even euphoria, but it isn't based on reality. You can't read their soul or make them do what you want. It's an illusion created from a high level of understanding about that player. You're able to play this well against them because you have the skill and experience to know a weaker player better than they know themselves—not because you have the power to read their soul. On the flip side, when you're losing, it can feel as if you're getting owned. *For more, go to page 144.*

2. **No Respect.** You can't control what people think of you, just as they can't control what you think of them. This is an illusion that's broken down on *page 138.*

Illusions about variance. The illusion that you can control variance makes you think that it's possible to have an influence over the cards themselves. You might overplay draws or overcall with small pocket pairs because you fully expect to hit. You might try to influence the action by calling out the cards you want, or clinging onto a good luck charm. On the other hand, you might get pessimistic and anticipate getting sucked out on, or fold strong hands because you assume you will be coolered. The following sections can help you to resolve the underlying flaws that create this illusion:

1. **Money Lost.** The illusion that the money you lose in a session is gone forever is corrected on *page 112.*

2. **Predicting Bad Beats.** The mind has the ability to predict the future. However, players often think that a bad beat happens because they think one is coming. *See page 92 for more.*

3. **Being Above Variance.** Players with entitlement tilt often think they should always win against weaker players. In order to believe that, they must also believe that the rules of variance don't apply to them. *See page 129 for more.*

INJECTING LOGIC **BELIEVING THAT YOU COULDN'T LOSE TO A FISH DOESN'T CHANGE THE FACT THAT YOU DID.**

CLIENT'S STORY

Matt "mbolt1" Bolt
$3/$6 to $50/$100 NLHE

DRAGTHEBAR COACH

"When I was winning, I expected to win $5,000 or $10,000 every day, but sooner or later I would have a day where I would lose a Range Rover and it would be a disaster. The highs would be very high, I would feel invincible—and the lows were very low, I would feel helpless. Even though I knew I was good enough to be playing high stakes, it would get so bad I would question if I was ever a winning player, and whether I would ever win again. This cycle happened every three or four months for over a year. I always would assume I would get lucky and get it back. Then sooner or later there would be no money left in my account . . . good game . . . Jared I need you.

Jared made me really focus not on how I was running, but on how I was playing. Now even when I'm running good, I try and stay focused on one hand at a time. When I get overconfident, I nip it in the bud early. It's really hard to recognize when you are not playing your best. When you write down your signs of overconfidence, it's easier to prevent it from happening. When I start opening wider (65 suited under the gun) and don't fold to 3-bets, I automatically know I am overconfident.

It's pretty cool, because reducing overconfidence also makes it easier to stay in a good state of mind when it goes bad. The tilt fuse gets longer and my tolerance for losing increases, because I know how I'm playing then too. So the highs are never as high and the lows no longer as low. It's also way easier to leave poker at the computer. It used to be that if I had a bad poker day, I had a bad life day and it would affect me away from the tables. The more balanced approach lets you separate poker from your life."

YOU CAN'T CONTROL THE CARDS; YOU CAN ONLY CONTROL HOW YOU PLAY.

DON'T GIVE UP CONTROL FOR SOMETHING YOU CAN'T CONTROL.

Illusion of Permanence

Confidence problems are created when you believe the illusion that the constantly changing aspects of poker somehow won't change in the future. For example, when you're running terribly, you assume it will never end. When you are running hot, it's just a matter of time before you are playing up at Rail Heaven. In both scenarios, the illusion that what's happening now continues indefinitely into the future fuels intense emotions. It's as if you've pressed the repeat button on the present, or what you're imagining in the present, and it just continues to play out that way in the future. A great run or a terrible run is assumed to continue, so your confidence artificially increases or decreases.

This is flawed because poker is a dynamic game that is constantly changing. For example, many internet players during the Moneymaker/ PartyPoker days assumed the games would continue to be soft. They got complacent, stopped working on their game, and got lapped by players who worked harder. If you fail to keep up with the changing dynamics in the game, like them you also could end up out of the game.

Assuming your opponents won't adjust is another example of this illusion. If you were getting destroyed by the same player over a good sample, you'd work hard to figure out why, so you could play better against them. You're not going to give up and just passively keep showing up to get your ass handed to you. Yet that's what you're assuming your opponents are going to do. If you expect to keep destroying the same player and then they start beating you, you'll just brush it off as variance without considering that they may now have an edge on you. *For more, see page 132.*

Here are some other flaws that create the illusion of permanence:

1. **Expecting to always play your A-game.** Your A-game is a moving target. As you improve, your A-game also advances. Playing your best all the time is possible, though still difficult even if you consistently and aggressively work to improve your game. However, the players who tend to struggle with this flaw believe playing their A-game is something they can expect. So they show up at the table having done very little, if any, work on their game and expect their best to just show up.

    Unconscious Competence is the only part of your skill set you can expect to show up by doing nothing other than sitting down at the table. Everything else is in the process of being learned and requires focus and thought to perform correctly. However, if you expect to play your A-game without putting in the energy at and away from the table, you're signaling to your brain not to focus on the skills currently being learned. You believe your A-game is automatic, so you presume that all the skills being learned are automatic as well. By expecting to play your best, it's practically guaranteed that you won't.

THINKING POKER IS THIS EASY HAS TO BE A DREAM, SO KEEP WORKING.

2. **Potential vs. Actual.** Your potential is what you believe you're capable of achieving. Your actual skill or results is what you have already achieved. When players believe their potential is already proven, their confidence artificially increases because these imagined results produce feelings of confidence in a similar way as real results. Since these results haven't been proven yet, it doesn't take much to expose the truth. Even just one losing session is enough.

The flaw here is subtle, yet it causes so many problems. Having a strong belief in your game is a great thing—it's recognition of your potential. However, the illusion is that you already *know* that you should be winning more, crushing the next limit, or having won a big tournament. You believe so deeply that this will be true, that part of your confidence is now built upon future results that you can't prove yet.

Until you have enough results, knowledge, and experience to prove that you have realized your potential, dial back your level of certainty and keep working.

Illusion of Learning

If you previously were unfamiliar with the ALM, inchworm, or the process model, you may have developed errors in your beliefs about learning. These errors often create confidence problems, and correcting them is necessary to have stable confidence.

All of the subsections within mistake tilt are examples of flaws that create illusions of learning. Here are the most common ones:

1. **Expecting perfection.** Believing you should not make mistakes can cause you to question your game when you inevitably make them. Having the goal of playing perfectly is fine, but expecting perfection means you'll have no tolerance for mistakes or the reality of the learning process. When playing or running great, it's easy to feel like you're no longer going to make mistakes, but that illusion leaves you blind to the real ones being made. Conversely, when playing or running badly, you'll feel much worse about your game relative to the severity of your mistakes. *See page 119 for more.*

2. **Premature mastery.** When on a good run of cards or during a streak of great play, it's easy to be fooled into thinking that

areas of your game that you are currently learning (Conscious Competence) are actually learned to the level of Unconscious Competence. Believing this subtle illusion means you'll stop working on the parts of your game that were in the process of being learned. Unfortunately, you're now expecting this part of your game to be automatic, but it's not. Since you're not focusing on this area, you make mistakes, and not knowing why you made them causes your confidence and motivation to take a hit.

A given skill is mastered only when consistently performed under intense pressure. If this isn't the case, keep working on this skill until it's proven to consistently show up under pressure.

 ESTIMATE WHAT YOU'VE MASTERED UNTIL IT'S PROVEN UNDER INTENSE PRESSURE.

Wishing

Wishing is a critical factor that can undermine not only confidence, but also your ability to correct any of these illusions. It is one thing to get fooled into thinking these illusions are real; it's quite another to actually wish they were real. Breaking these illusions is impossible when you wish you could just sit down and print money, that there was no variance in poker, or that you could always play perfect poker.

When you have wishes such as these, it means that you're holding out hope that one day they could come true. Why would you work hard to correct problems in your poker or mental game, when deep down you wish they could all go away by snapping your fingers? If you believe a poker genie is going to grant you the wish of eternal run good, it would be illogical to work hard on your game.

Spotting these wishes can be tough, so here's a simple way of testing if you're harboring them. Answer honestly:

- Do you want to win every hand? Or even think it would be cool if you could?
- Do you wish you could control the cards?
- Do you wish poker would always be like it is when you're running well?
- Do you wish there was no variance in poker?

These and other wishes must be eliminated in order to resolve the illusions causing under- and overconfidence. To do that:

1. Prove logically why you don't want your wishes to come true.
2. Describe the consequences believing in these wishes has on your game.
3. Describe what you would get by having your wishes come true. Then devise a strategy to achieve your wishes in a real way.

These wishes can never come true. Believing in them is no different from believing in Santa Claus. Eliminate them, and you'll be in a great position to develop stable confidence and a strong poker and mental game—and ultimately, you'll have more success in poker.

CLIENT'S STORY

Sean Gibson
$1/$2 NLHE Full Ring

POKER NEWS DAILY

"My story is probably very familiar. I made a $250 deposit online, quickly blew through the micro stakes, and before I knew it, I jumped into the 200NL games looking to take my game to the next level. Then in January of 2010, I hit a wall in the form of a huge downswing, 22 buy-ins straight down. I lost my confidence, and with it, my will to play. I went from thinking I could hang with the pros and making a nice side income, to just suddenly not playing. In five months I played 50,000 hands, which is normally in the neighborhood of what I play in a month.

I felt like I was at the bottom of the barrel when I first talked to Jared. I felt cursed—not just in poker, but I was running bad in aspects of life, too. That came up in our sessions, and I felt ridiculous bringing it up, but there it was. Ironically, my problems at the table mirrored those away from it, and Jared helped me to see that it had a lot to do with how I handled variance.

When I tilt, I insta-quit; hence my five months of low volume. The variance was truly unbelievable—almost everything that could happen did, and I'd often say out loud while playing, 'I don't believe it' or 'That's unbelievable' to the perceived ridiculous things happening to me. Jared helped me realize that if it's within the boundaries of the rules, it can happen, and it will happen over the course of millions of hands. The logic statement, 'It must be possible if it happened, was really powerful for me. I accepted that statement as a fundamental truth, and the tilt has faded because now I'm ready for the variance and accept it.

Strangely enough, part of what made dealing with variance tougher was that a part of me wished I could control it. No one wants to deal with negative variance—who wouldn't want to run good all the time?—but I had no idea that wishing made me less likely to figure out how to handle it better. He helped me realize that if my wish came true and I could control variance, poker would become intolerably boring. The irony here is that I hated poker for the very reason I loved it; and because of that, would stop playing due to the variance that actually makes the game so much more enjoyable over no-variance ones like chess. Really understanding that made dealing with variance much more tolerable.

He also pointed out a lot of the layers of what a poker player goes through mentally that can really damage their confidence, ability, and drive to succeed. Now, I set daily volume goals, where before I would quit when I didn't feel like playing. Physically writing down my goals and having them in front of me is really important; I do it every day. I have to keep putting the hands in, and now if I feel like quitting before I have reached my goal, I'll keep playing until I do.

Although we've just begun our journey together, Jared Tendler helped me understand the roots of my frustrations, rather than giving me parlor tricks on how to fend them off. I simply couldn't have asked for a better way to approach my mental game."

CONCLUSION

YOU HAVE NOT MASTERED
THE MENTAL GAME

HAVING FINISHED THE BOOK, you may think you have mastered the mental game. You haven't yet. It's not possible to develop mental game skill to the level of Unconscious Competence that quickly. Instead, take what you've learned so far, put it into action, and gain some experience to see what has stuck and what needs more work.

At some point, expect that you'll fall back into old habits and go on insane monkey tilt, have your mind go totally blank in a huge pot, or get totally demoralized during a rough stretch of cards. Even if improvement happens quickly, there are still setbacks, struggles, and mistakes along the way. Steps backward are part of the learning process; they're going to happen at some point. When they do, use this book to help you to continue making progress.

There are no magic cures to real mental game problems. If you want to improve, you have to put in the work. Sure, it's going to come easier for some players than others. So what? If you have goals you want to achieve in poker, don't let tilt, fear, motivation, or confidence problems deter you. The reward is out there right now for those players willing to do what's necessary. The answers are now in your hands, but if you have questions, come find me on the forums or at www.JaredTendlerPoker.com.

APPENDIX 1

WARM-UP AND COOL-DOWN

IN EVERY MAJOR SPORT, professionals and serious players have some form of a structured warm-up and cool-down immediately before and after they play. In general, poker players aren't convinced yet of why this is so important to them, nor is there much information available on how best to do it.

The greatest predictor of long-term success is learning and improving every day.

Your job is to continue to stay a step ahead of your opponents. You can do that by making sure you're ready to play better (even if just slightly) each day you play. A structured warm-up and cool-down is one of the easiest ways to consistently play at a higher level.

Playing at higher levels means you are continually learning. As the ALM shows, the learning process has many levels and a lot of repetition and experience is needed to learn a skill to the level of Unconscious Competence. Warming up and cooling down help you identify what to improve, and help you keep a close eye on your progress. Warming up what you're currently in the process of learning makes these skills more likely to show up while you're playing. Playing poker is a great training ground, and when you can consistently perform, for example, proper

3-bet frequency or tilt control, you get in the necessary repetitions to learn a skill to the level of Unconscious Competence.

Cooling down helps you to put poker down and relax. Playing poker can be intense, so think of cooling down as the equivalent of icing your muscles after a tough game. In mental terms, this means that you're evaluating how you played, keeping track of your progress, and identifying anything new that you learned.

Warm-Up

If the concept of warming up before you play is new, start with a basic three-minute version. As you get used to doing a warm-up, add additional strategies so you're ready to play at a high level when you first start playing. There is a limit to how much time you should spend warming up. In general, anything around 15 minutes is about right. Of course, if more time works well for you, do it.

Basic three-minute warm-up

1. **Review what you are working on.** Remind yourself of a few things in your game that you're trying to improve. Do this by briefly reviewing some specific technical improvements in your poker skill, such as value betting more, tightening up your opening range, or 3-betting less. Also review the strategy you're using to improve mental game problems.

2. **Take a few deep breaths to focus and go play.**

Additional warm-up strategies

*   Decide how long you're going to play. Having a set time makes poker more structured and for many players that makes their mental game stronger. Obviously you can adjust depending on the quality of the games.

- Remove any non-poker related distractions, including your phone, chat, TV, other people, and random internet browsers.

- Review your long-term goals.

- Take notes on anything that's weighing on your mind from your personal life. That way you can focus entirely on playing and easily pick these things back up afterward.

- Review hand histories that fit with what you are currently improving. You can do the same for a mental game problem by reviewing mental hand histories, or anything else you've written about that problem.

- Many players watch poker training videos before they play. That's best only if you already watched the video and it fits with the parts of your game you're trying to improve. In this way, the video refreshes your memory, rather than teaching you something entirely new. Before you start playing is not the time to learn, it's the time to reinforce what you are learning so you're more likely to execute it while playing.

- Exercise or go for a walk.

- Try meditating, visualizing, or breathing exercises.

- Play 30% to 50% of your usual number of tables for 30 minutes. Consider this to be an extended warm-up that's designed to create a bridge between warming up and playing. Playing a fraction of the tables allows you to think more about the concepts you're trying to improve, steadily get into the flow of the action, and get in the best frame of mind before really grinding.

Cool-down

As with the warm-up, if cooling down is new to you, consider starting with this three-minute version. Then as you get used to doing it more, incorporate additional strategies to make it even more effective.

Basic three-minute cool-down

1. **Estimate variance.** Since you can't rely entirely on results in the short term, you need a more objective way of identifying how you played. That starts by estimating the effect variance had on your results.

2. **Evaluate how you played.** Get a sense of how you did in the areas of your game, technical or mental, that you are trying to improve. Were you able to stop yourself from tilting or spot the signs of tilt sooner? If not, what happened? Did you rectify previous technical mistakes? If not, what happened?

Additional cool-down strategies

- Marking hands during the session makes it easier to review your play afterwards. Unsure what hands to mark during your sessions? Choose non-standard hands where your decision was tough, where you thought you may have made a mistake, where tilt started to show up, where you made a creative move, or other spots that can help you learn and determine how you played. Then after the session, review those hands. That doesn't mean you need to get into a hardcore analysis, but at least take some game flow notes so you can analyze those hands in context when working on them later.

- Take notes about any new details of your mental game problems and add them to your profile.

- Take a note of anything new that you did well. This can indicate ways to improve your game even more in the future.

- Look closely at how the regulars played and make notes for the future.

- Productively vent by writing about whatever is weighing on your mind.

- Refine your next warm-up based on what you found in this session.

APPENDIX II

CLIENT QUESTIONNAIRE

PRIOR TO THEIR FIRST coaching session, clients answer the questions listed on the next few pages. Although some questions may seem redundant, asking overlapping questions is important to properly assess all areas of the mental game. Many clients say that filling out the questionnaire helps them to increase recognition of their problems, and makes improving their mental game easier.

When clients answer the questionnaire, they also follow these instructions:

First phase. Write down _only_ the answers that come easily to you. If you are having a difficult time answering a question or believe that it's not relevant to you, skip it and go to the next one. Begin these answers with the notation **(1ˢᵗ) in bold**.

Second phase. For each question that was skipped in the first phase, provide an answer. Begin these answers with the notation **(2ⁿᵈ) in bold**.

Third phase. Three to five days after completing the questionnaire, read through each of your answers and _only_ add anything _new_ that comes to mind. Begin these answers with the notation **(3ʳᵈ) in bold**.

If going over the questionnaire three times seems excessive, here's the rationale:

- The first phase defines what you already know well.
- The second phase forces you to think harder.
- The third phase gives you the opportunity to identify new details that weren't originally on your mind. Details matter a lot when resolving mental game problems, and digging additional ones out of your head can make a big difference in how quickly you improve.

1. First share a bit about yourself (education, interests, family, etc):

2. Briefly describe your poker history. How would you characterize your progress? What game(s)/limit(s) do you play?

3. What are your goals in poker? Short- and long-term.

4. What personal goals does poker support?

5. List and describe the problems in your mental game. List them in order of importance to you or by severity. Give as much information as you can, including the triggers, signs, and what you believe are the causes.

6. What have you tried to do to fix any of these issues? What level of success have you had?

7. Do factors outside of poker ever affect your play? If yes, how? Does poker ever negatively impact your life? If yes, how?

8. Why do you play poker? What motivates you to play, why do you love it, what do you get out of it?

9. List your three to five biggest distractions while playing. Describe why these are a problem.

10. How do you decide when to play? Do you have set times or is it flexible or random?

11. Describe what you do before you play. How do you warm up, if you do?

12. What is your average session length?
How many sessions do you play per day?
How many hours do you play per month on average?
Are any of these shorter than your goal? If so, in what ways are the problems listed in question 5 related?

13. What are the reasons that you would quit a session prematurely? Are the problems listed in question 5 ever the cause?

14. Describe your work ethic. Is procrastination or burnout ever a problem?

15. Describe what you do away from the table to improve technically as a player.

16. Do you ever act without thinking in a way that's negative? If yes, why? What is the typical situation when it happens?

17. Describe your mindset when you are playing your best.

18. Do you ever get down about your ability as a player? If so, can it happen after one bad session?

19. How well do you typically handle pressure situations in poker or elsewhere (if different than poker)? Describe.

20. Do you have any specific memories in poker that you still think about or that pop into your head randomly? (Bad hands, tournament bust outs, or others.)

21. Does thinking about poker ever keep you up at night, or prevent you from enjoying your life? If so, what are you thinking about? Do you ever get stuck thinking about mistakes?

22. Hypothetical question: You have the ability to magically make any of the issues in question 5 disappear. Which one would you choose? Why? What do you think your game would be like without it?

23. List and/or describe your mental strengths.

24. Do you take notes on your game after a session? If yes, describe.

25. How much is your evaluation of your ability as a player influenced by results? Describe.

26. Do you exercise? If yes, on average how often and generally what do you do?

27. How much do you sleep on average per night? Is sleep ever an issue? If so, describe. What, if anything, do you notice about your play on days when you don't sleep well or long enough?

28. Do you eat or drink anything when playing? If yes, describe what is typical.

29. Do you smoke cigarettes, drink alcohol, or use any other drugs when playing? If yes, what and how much on average? What effect, positive or negative, do you think it has on your game?

30. Do you have any medical illnesses at this time? If yes, how does it affect any of the issues in question 5?

31. Do you have any current psychological issues that have been diagnosed by a doctor or someone in the psychological field? If yes, what, if anything, is your current treatment and how do you think it affects any of the issues in question 5?

32. Estimate the amount lost per month as a result of the problems you want to address. Also estimate the percent of time you play your A-game.

Jared Tendler, M.S., LMHC, was a mental game coach for golfers on the PGA and LPGA tours before he became the leading mental game expert in poker. He now coaches more than 300 poker professionals, including some of the top players in the world. Jared's groundbreaking methods have also helped thousands more through his training videos, articles, and forum Q&As. Jared earned a master's degree in Counseling Psychology from Northeastern University, and became a licensed mental health counselor prior to becoming a mental game coach in 2005. For more information about Jared's coaching, or to check out his latest podcast, article, and blog go to: www.jaredtendlerpoker.com. You can follow him on Twitter: @JaredTendler or at Facebook.com/jaredtendlerpoker.

Barry's photo courtesy of Mickey May and BoylePoker.

Barry Carter is a poker player and the news editor at Poker Strategy.com. He would like to make it known that his role in this book was primarily to provide a poker player's voice to Jared's work—he didn't create the theories themselves. He lives in Sheffield, England, with his wife Gina and their dog Charlie. You can find out more at: www.pokermediapro.com. And follow him @Barry_Carter on Twitter.

ALSO FROM JARED TENDLER

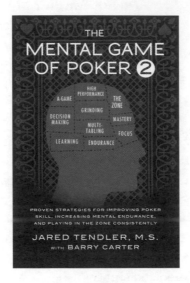

Imagine the edge you would have if you could consistently play poker in the zone. In the zone you make all the right decisions, instinctively when to bluff, and are unfazed by a losing hand. You're locked in and feel unbeatable. It's shocking how many poker players *stumble* into this elusive state of mind. As quickly as that euphoric feeling of invincibility arrives, it's gone. And no matter how hard they try, they can't get back there. Until now.

In *The Mental Game of Poker 2*, author and renowned poker mental game coach Jared Tendler breaks down the zone and delivers actionable steps to help players get there consistently. He demystifies the zone, and for the first time, brings logic and order to this previously misunderstood concept. This book provides proven strategies to:

- Play poker longer and across more online tables.
- Improve decision making.
- Learn faster.
- Eliminate C-game mistakes.
- Increase focus and discipline.